P9-BXY-514

Church Growth in Japan

ABOUT THE COVER: The carp is a symbol in Japan for Boy's Festival because it has the power to fight its way up swift streams and because of its determination to overcome obstacles. It is held to be a fitting example for growing boys, typifying, as it does, ambition, strength and the will to overcome difficulties. The Christian symbol of the *ichthus* (fish) has been substituted for the carp to demonstrate the struggling church in the land of the "rising sun."

Design by Agape Typesetting & Design,
Fullerton, California

Affectionately Dedicated

to

Judy, Kelli and Steven

Church Growth in Japan

A Study in the Development of
Eight Denominations
1859-1939

by

Tetsunao Yamamori

William Carey Library

SOUTH PASADENA, CALIF.

Copyright © 1974 by Tetsunao Yamamori

All rights reserved.

No part of this book may be used or reproduced in any manner whatsoever without written permission, except in the case of brief quotations
embodied in critical articles and reviews.

Library of Congress Cataloging in Publication Data

Yamamori, Tetsunao, 1937--
    Church growth in Japan

    Revised version of the author's thesis, Duke University.
    Bibliography: p.
    1. Protestant church--Japan.   2.   Church growth--Case studies.
I.   Title.
BR1305.Y35   28'.4'0952   74-4009
ISBN 0-87808-412-6

Published by the William Carey Library
533 Hermosa Street
South Pasadena, Calif. 91030
Telephone 213-799-4559

PRINTED IN THE UNITED STATES OF AMERICA

Table of Contents

87534

List of Tables

Foreword

Dr. Yamamori's is by all odds the most extensive, exact, and stimulating study available of church growth in Japan. It should be mastered by every minister and missionary there and translated into Japanese as soon as possible, so that Christian thinking about the evangelization of Japan can be done in view of the facts. Only a poor devotion scorns knowledge. Those who desire most to be good stewards of God's grace will be keenest to understand the complex processes by which the Gospel has been proclaimed and believed and churches have risen and spread across the island nation.

Years of Dr. Yamamori's life have gone into this book. He dug out the membership facts for each of the eight denominations and refined them. He compared the figures as given by Japanese headquarters with those given by American and English boards. His data base for these eighty years is impeccable. He read everything available on Japanese culture and history. He pored over biographies of noted Japanese Christian leaders and missionaries. He analyzed books and articles published by missionary societies. Then he spent six months in Japan — he grew up there and speaks and reads Japanese as readily as English — studying Japanese writings bearing on the acceptance and rejection of the Gospel. He interviewed notable Christians who knew the situation first hand and tested his hypotheses on them.

Of special importance is Chapter V, in which he describes the two decades between the wars — 1919 to 1939. The first decade was favorable to church growth and the second was hostile to it. What the eight Churches achieved during these contrasting decades is significant. In this chapter Yamamori introduces a ninth Church which began only in 1917 and started to grow only in 1924. Then during eight wonderful years (1925-1932) it grew from 3,000 to 20,000! He contrasts the 'school approach' used by the eight Churches with the 'conversion approach' used by the ninth Church — with illuminating results.

Church Growth in Japan harnesses the best insights of sociology and history to the propagation of the Gospel. The study is sound, the methodology competent, and the scope limited enough to permit a thorough treatment. The findings will stand. The book will be avidly read in Japan. It should be read by those in other nations also who wish to be more effective in communicating the faith.

February 1st, 1973

Donald McGavran
School of Missions and
      Institute of Church Growth
Fuller Theological Seminary.
Pasadena, California

Acknowledgments

Church Growth in Japan was originally written in partial fulfill-
ment for a doctorate at Duke University. William Carey Library has
now kindly brought this to book form with minor changes.

It is impossible to mention everyone who has helped me along the
way in the preparation of this book. I do wish, however, to acknowledge by category those who rendered their ready assistance to me.
In Japan, I wish to thank the scholars, pastors, and laymen who
responded to my interviews; the retired and active missionaries to
Japan, without whose dedication and endless striving there would
be no church growth; and my colleagues at Doshisha University in
Kyoto. In America, I would like to thank the officials at the various
denominational mission headquarters and archives; the professors
at Duke University who supervised my dissertation; and Mr. Patrick
Bennett of McMurry College, Mrs. Jack Nipper of Milligan College,
Dr. Ralph Winter of William Carey Library, and Judy, my wife, for
their valuable editorial suggestions.

T.Y.

Introduction

Just how does the church grow in a predominantly non-Christian culture? More precisely, why do some churches (denominations) grow faster than others in some sector of society over certain periods of history? These and similar questions often puzzle the minds of many Christians in Japan and elsewhere. Should these be properly answered, they would cast light upon those factors which are functional as well as dysfunctional to the growth of the Christian faith and other religions; they would have scientific value. The purpose of this book, then, is to describe and analyze the growth and development of eight Protestant churches founded in Japan before 1900. The present case study aims at scrutinizing the factors which made for the growth, or non-growth, of these churches for the period between 1859 and 1939. This is not, however, a complete history of these churches, but it is historical in its approach. Neither is this a comprehensive study of Japanese society, but it is sociological in its use of material and its analysis. Indeed, this is a historical and sociological study of Japanese Protestantism (in its limited scope) from the point of view of its growth and development. The eight selected churches are: (1) The Nippon Seikokai (Episcopal —Anglican); (2) The Nippon Kirisuto Kyokai (Presbyterian); (3) The American Baptist Church (ABFMS); (4) The Kumiai Kyokai (Congregational); (5) The Nippon Mesodesuto Kyokai (Methodist); (6) The Christian Churches (Disciples of Christ); (7) The Southern Baptist Church; and (8) The Seventh-Day Adventist Church.

The successful implementation of the purpose set forth in this dissertation largely depends upon the method utilized to achieve the desired goal. The methodology,[1] therefore, must be stated accurately and in detail. The methodological procedure has two major steps.

1. Measuring church growth. The capacity to measure something is predicated on the assumption that the subject of measurement will yield to the principle of measurement; something to be measured must be objectively measurable. This may sound too simplistic, but when the principle is applied to the matter of church growth, the picture suddenly changes; it is not at all clear. Whether the growth of the church should or should not be measured is to be debated elsewhere. Here we are concerned with the prior question of whether or not it *can* be measured. The writer judges that it can be.

First, the terms "church" and "growth" must be defined. The term "church" is variously defined for different purposes. The definition ranges from the strict theological interpretation to the sociological. Theologically, the meaning of "church" is used "in no less than six different senses."[2] Sociologically, the church may be defined as "a man-made institution" in the sense that it is "*a set of human relationships organized to facilitate adaptation to the Unknown.*"[3] The church, as a divine society, draws its inner courage from the grace of God revealed in Christ and constantly made available by the Holy Spirit. It nevertheless exists in time and space and is composed of men and women vulnerable to human influence and environment. In other words, the church, among other things, is a sociological entity subject to analysis by the principles used in the study of all other human institutions. The church, according to Best, may be said to possess at least three characteristics: an expressed body of belief, some form of organization, and a constituency.[4] Any social group has its creed, organization, and membership; the church, at least in its sociological aspect, differs little from any other social group. Only by defining the church as being made up of *concrete* individuals taking part in the society at large, the study of *church* growth becomes possible.

We now turn to the meaning of "growth". When we speak of the growth of the church in this study, we are thinking in terms of increase of membership constituency composed of men and women who can be counted. Admittedly, this is not the only way in which the church is commonly known to grow. For example, the church, like any social group, grows in its creedal and organizational aspects which are pursued primarily by the theologians and historians of the church. While these aspects receive our attention insofar as they influenced the physical expansion of the church, they do not serve our purpose of becoming the objective criterion by which the growth of the church is measured. They inevitably involve theological and ecclesiastical value judgments which would cause never-ending arguments centering on the nature of the church and the norms of the Christian faith. In addition, the members of the church are said to grow qualitatively in patience, humility, kindness, obedience, faithfulness, hope, and love. These are the qualities which are measured only by God. These will no doubt influence the kinds of numerical growth obtained, but they themselves cannot be the criteria by which church growth is measured.

Having specified the meaning of "growth", we are confronted with a further difficulty: who among the members should be counted? Nida states the problem succinctly when he writes:

> Even if we restrict ourselves to so-called statistical growth, we really do not know how to count, for in the opinion of some persons one must count only baptized believers (that is, adults), while other church leaders insist that if one is to obtain an accurate view of the significance of the Christian witness it is not only legitimate but necessary to count the total number of persons in the Christian community.[5]

The problem will be intensified when we realize that there are, within the church, members who, according to their religious participation, might be grouped as "nuclear" (most active) at one extreme pole of the scale and as "marginal" (least active) at the other.[6]

Are we justified in counting only the baptized adults and not their dependents? Or should the criterion of comparing the growth of one church with that of another be based on the size of only the nuclear members who constitute the very core of any church? What category of membership (in the face of this obvious confusion) must we use as the standard of measurement? Fortunately, there is a category of membership which has a long and honorable history as the best single measure of the size of a denomination. "Communicants" is the word and category used by missionary statisticians who compiled *World Atlas of Christian Missions* (1911), *World Missionary Atlas* (1925), and *Interpretative Statistical Survey of the World Mission* (1938).[7] In these three books, "communicants" is a technical term meaning "*baptized members in good standing.*" This category does not include catechumena, inquirers, sympathizers, church attenders who are not baptized believers, or infants who have been baptized. The "communicants" of the 'paedo-baptist' denominations and the "members" of the baptist denominations are roughly comparable. The writer uses this word in this meaning.

The problem put forth by Nida may be more clearly elucidated when we distinguish between community and communicants.

Any denomination consists of the communicants plus their intimate dependents. Communicants have babies who are Christian, not Buddhist or Shintoist babies. Communicants sometimes grow cold, quit coming to church, or never contribute to the church. Yet when asked if they are Buddhist, Shintoist, or Christian, they identify themselves as Christian. Communicants have aged parents, widowed daughters, and sometimes servants or other dependents who attend church and count themselves as Christians but are not full members. Some denominations seek out and baptize these infants and dependents, and keep their names on the roll even if they are inactive for a long period. These denominations say that they report only the baptized, but they baptize very many infants. Other denominations baptize only after much instruction. Whatever they do, both kinds of denominations have intimate dependents who count themselves in some way as Christians. *The communicants plus intimate dependents make up the Christian community.*

The Episcopal Church in Japan, for example, has for forty years recorded membership under four headings:[8] (1) Active Communicants — adult members only who commune at least once a year; (2) Total Communicants — adult members only who are entitled to commune if they choose to; (3) Active Members — members, infant or adult, who have been baptized and take some part in the life of the church; and (4) Total Members — total *registered* members including baptized infants and adult members, active or inactive, known or unknown.

Let us look at the record for 1938:

Active Communicants	Total Communicants	Active Members	Total Members
11,605	18,192	28,606	47,244

The figure which missionary statisticians through the years have used and are using today[9] is Total Communicants — 18,192 in this case. This category would include, in Fichter's terminology, "nuclear", "modal", and to a certain degree, "marginal" members (communicants) within the church. (Factors like keeping inactives on the list affect all churches alike.) This entity comprising the category of Total Communicants is the best available set of figures which will form the basis of comparative analysis of church growth. But it must be added that a community of 47,244 (about 2.5 times as large as 18,192) is also an important figure.[10]

What is meant by "church growth" has been thus far explicated. It is made clear that the growth of the church can be measured on the basis of numerical increase of communicants. In order to measure church growth or to pinpoint specific periods of growth or decline among the eight churches, the writer constructed Figure 1 (p. 6) as a measuring device. The vertical scale indicates communicants and the horizontal base shows the chronology in decades. The graph vividly portrays how these churches grew in Japan.

The accuracy of Figure 1 (p. 6) in painting the growth picture depends upon the reliability of the figures. Utmost care has been taken in compiling the facts; getting them was a long, complex process.[11] Archives in Japan, America, and Canada have been combed. The writer presents these figures as the best available. But the question must still be asked: are the lines of growth shown on the graph reliable? The answer is affirmative. The official figure for a given year may be in minor error, for any one of a number of causes. But the general trend of growth is highly reliable. The succession of figures cannot be in error; a mistake made in one year will be corrected in the next.

Once in a while, however, the written material proves the graph "wrong". The graph may be "wrong" in that the figure reported is a statistical redefinition. It may be "wrong" in that the figure reported is a typographical error. Furthermore, it may be "wrong" in that the figure reported shows a split or a merger. By cross-examining the written material, the figures must be refined and correctly interpreted.

In the main, Figure 1[12] (p. 6) portrays a fair picture of the trends of growth of eight churches. Whatever the margin of error, it is far better to discuss the dynamics of church growth in Japan against the graph than against subjective factors.

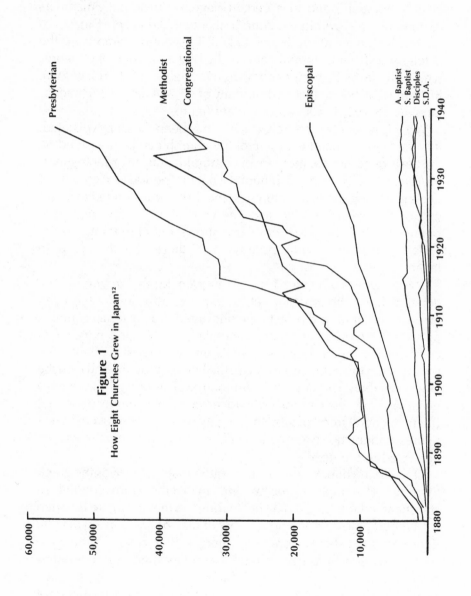

Figure 1
How Eight Churches Grew in Japan[12]

2. Testing the causes against the graph. The primary purpose of compiling communicant membership (through a long and arduous effort) and of constructing Figure 1 (p. 6) as a measuring device was to discover and test the causes of growth against the actual growth. With the graph of growth before him, one can not only see the ups and downs within the history of one church but also compare the growth of that church with the growth obtained by other churches. Figure 1 (p. 6) is rich in comparison. Mission and church records are full of alleged reasons for the growth and for the non-growth. Failure to have the accurate graph of growth leaves the mission executive or church official open to the wrong interpretation of growth history of his church. Our practice of constantly referring to the graph and testing the causes against the actual growth saves us from committing the error of giving wrong reasons for growth or decline. By comparing the growth of one church with that of another, alleged reasons may be further eliminated and a truer picture of church growth procured. For example, the mission policy of dispersing the missionary force (over against the theory of concentration in a few key areas) which actually produced the sizable growth of one church does not necessarily affect another church the same way. Different internal and external circumstances of the church must be considered. Or an environmental factor such as anti-Westernism evokes different patterns of response from different churches resulting in different patterns of growth. In this case, the question must be asked: to what extent and under what circumstances do environmental factors affect church growth?

Throughout our study, we encountered innumerable possible causes of the growth of these churches. The key which hopefully saved us from our misrepresentation was the practice of always testing the probable factors against the actual growth. There are four main sources of information which we utilized.

First, theses and dissertations which had the slightest bearing on the church in Japan have been studied. Among many, those written by Thomas[13] and Copeland[14] proved to be most helpful. The former deals more directly with the subject of church growth for the period 1883-1889, while the latter sets the context for the discussion of retarded growth for the decade after 1890. The writer is personally indebted to these men for their encouragement and works of scholarly competence. Other theses and dissertations whose primary purposes were other than church growth study also merited close inquiry.

Second, mission and church publications formed an indispensable source of information for this study. The writer spent almost two months in the summer of 1968 visiting the mission archives and depositories of the eight churches located from as far north as Cambridge, Massachusetts to as far south as Austin, Texas. He read extensively the minutes and records meticulously kept by the mission secretary for the possible change in mission policy. Then he critically analyzed the explanations of slow growth of one church given by its field executive in a paper delivered to its Board meeting. He combed through the annual reports and the files of correspondence between the missionaries and their superiors at the mission headquarters. Then he was delighted to discover some old pamphlets and books not available anywhere else. In all these places, the results of the investigaion were not always commensurate with the labor put in, but there emerged many insights which later led him to important discoveries.

Third, a body of information which may be categorized as "secular publications" consists of census reports and studies by the Japanese Government and articles and books by anthropologists and sociologists, both Japanese and Western. These writings complemented the churchly data in interpreting the impact of the social and cultural *milieu* upon the processes of growth and development of eight churches.

Fourth, the writer spent the academic year 1968-69 in Kyoto, Japan doing his field research. His project there was divided into three parts: (1) gathering data at The Institute of Christianity and Social Problems, Doshisha University, (2) interviews; (3) a detailed survey of "Ten Kyodan Churches in Kyoto." Doshisha University, with help from The Yen-Ching Institute of Harvard University, established The Institute of Christianity and Social Problems a few years ago. The Institute, possibly more than any other institution in Japan, possesses extensive holdings on the Japanese church related to the period of this study. Scholars connected with it were most cordial and of great assistance to this researcher. Kyoto, rich in tradition and sensitive to the changing ways of Japanese life, became the base of operation for the field work. The writer spent countless hours examining the old documents and massive data written in and preserved for the past century.

Interviews with the persons knowledgeable of the church life in Japan constitute another prime source for a study of this kind. Some one hundred nationals (both clergy and laity), missionaries, and scholars were consulted. Most of these were there before 1940 as active participants of the church. The astute observations of many of these persons on the causes of growth offered an invaluable understanding of the Japanese church. Not only has he gained knowledge of the church there through the testimonies of these eyewitnesses but also he has experienced firsthand the life of the church by sharing in services of worship and in moments of church fellowship. In seeking interviews, the writer travelled extensively and had the opportunity to see a variety of churches and their activities of both formal and informal nature. Many battles of church growth have been and are being fought at the level of local churches; the church grows, as a matter of fact, only when the local churches grow in their memberships. The moods and the patterns of fellowship and worship which prevail in the church life affect the growth. The writer was extremely fortunate to have facility in the Japanese language, so that he could detect the heartbeat of the local church life. His acquaintance with the delicate moods of dozens of local churches, widely scattered throughout Japan, furnished him with a sound basis on which to evaluate the data in their relationship to growth.

At one point in his stay in Japan, the writer conducted a depth study of ten selected Kyodan churches in Kyoto. What was discovered in this survey will be introduced and discussed in Chapter V.

In the preceding pages, we have stated the purpose and methodology of this dissertation. It remains to be seen how historical periods are divided and chapters organized in what follows.

The scholar rightly concerns himself with the way in which he divides historical periods. In discussing the history of Japanese Protestantism, there have emerged two dominant methods of periodization. One method adheres to the division of periods strictly according to events within church history. Ikado calls it "classical" and says that it has been used by both missionary and national scholars of prewar Japan.[15] The other incorporates the events of political and economic history with those of Japanese Protestantism. This, according to Ikado, has been the practice of scholars in postwar Japan. "This second classification," says he, "is better, since, using this, we can easily relate the historical events within the church to the history of the nation."[16] The writer concurs with him because the church, as a sociological entity subject to change by external forces, cannot remain unaffected by them. In our discussion of church growth, it seems inevitable that we take into consideration not only the events within the church but also those of national history. The periods in this book are chosen, therefore, by growth records plus the external and internal events of the church in Japan. There are five such periods: (1) the Exploratory Period (1859-1881); (2) Openness to the West (1882-1889); (3) the Hard Line (1890-1902); (4) Christian Resurgence (1903-1918); and (5) Between the Wars (1919-1939).

These periods of growth serve conveniently as chapter headings in this book. Each chapter is further divided into three sections: (1) socio-cultural setting; (2) ecclesiastical setting; and (3) church growth interpretation.

Section 1 sets forth the background of the soil in which the "miracle" of growth took place. Just as the seed planted in the ground manifests itself in various growth patterns depending on the quality and condition of the soil, the growth of a religion or a particular faith is influenced by various factors within the society which may facilitate or impede its developmental process. Church growth never occurs in a void; it cannot be understood without its social and cultural setting.

Section 2 describes the sower and the ways of seed-sowing. During the first eighty years of the Protestant mission in Japan, the Christian church tried many ways to propagate its faith. In each chapter of this study, there will be a brief mention of the church's activity — denominational beginnings, church mergers, evangelistic campaigns, and other notable happenings of ecclesiastical interest — as it related to the spread of the Christian faith. Inasmuch as the degree of membership increase is the basis of a later analysis, pertinent facts of growth granted to, or achieved by, the eight churches will be recorded in this section.

In Section 3, interpreting the interaction of multitudinous factors producing growth — rapid, slow, or stagnant, as the case may be — it is no simple matter to determine exactly which factors brought about specific results.

The sower, to continue our analogy, knows from his experience some of the ways in which he can cultivate the soil, plant the seed, water it, and continue to nurture it until it bears fruit. But what he does not know, having exhausted all that can possibly be done within the limits of his knowledge and experience, is why the seed grows or does not grow at all. There are many "imponderables" in the dynamics of growth beyond human knowing. In the case of church growth, there are both human and divine factors involved. The former set of factors is observable and can be put to test according to the principles of analysis applied to any scientific study of human institution, while the latter lies outside the boundary of technical knowledge. That the Holy Spirit is at work in granting growth to the churches is a legitimate Christian claim, but from the side of man it is impossible to separate the human from the divine. Section 3 devotes itself to the analysis of such human elements which made for the growth and obstruction of the church.

CHAPTER I

The Exploratory Period,
1859-1881

Socio-Cultural Setting

Each society of mankind has a structure of its own and recognizing it is a prerequisite to understanding church growth. The members of a society are not complete isolates separated from each other but are woven closely into some web relationships. The degree of tightness of these social relationships varies according to the geographical region or the particular sector of society. The way in which the society imposes its pattern of thinking or mode of behavior upon the individual member affects how the church grows in that society. A working hypothesis may be couched in the words of Joachim Wach, who wrote:

> Two factors appear to be essential in the development of a more highly individualistic religion: a gradual emancipation of the individual from the influence of his cultural and social background and a continuous process of differentiation within the civilization itself.[1]

The Christianity which was introduced to Japan for the first time in the mid-nineteenth century was highly individualistic. Therefore, our hypothesis may be stated as follows: the same two factors mentioned by Wach may be essential in the development of Japanese Protestantism between 1859 and 1939.

During the eighty-year period of this study, Japanese society went through much socio-cultural change and, through the process of industrialization, the civilization itself became gradually differentiated. The gravitational force in history seems to flow from one type of culture to another. Various phrases are used in the sociological literature to express this structural change in society from an essentially agrarian orientation to an industrial-urban one. Be it expressed in Töennies' *Gemeinschaft-Gesellschaft* dichotomous scheme[2], or in the "self versus collectivity orientations" of Parsons and Shils,[3] the fundamental change occurs in the relationship of the individual to his society. In a traditional agrarian society, the individual is swallowed up in group life where the communal principle dominates social relationships; he thinks, acts, and feels secure in a group. He gives priority to the interests and goals of his primary social groups such as his family and village. In a more industrialized society, the individual gradually becomes emancipated from tight-knit communal relationships. Such was the experience of the West, but whether this was so in the case of prewar Japan is to be examined later. The individual in such a society is no longer confined to the world based on kinship and neighborhood relations alone; his social life and family relationships become more atomized; in his work he is an individual hired on the contractual basis. More importantly, he is a rational will who thinks his own thoughts and acts on his own volition; he is a free man. It must be remembered, however, that whether it is an agrarian or industrial culture, both self and collectivity orientations are found there. But, as Kluckhohn rightly points out, it is a matter of emphasis.[4] In our study, the agrarian-industrial typology will serve as a useful framework and indicator against which socio-cultural changes of all sorts with levels of intensity may be detected as they influenced the growth of the Christian faith in Japan. In other words, we shall test our hypothesis (and essentially, that of Wach) and qualify it, if necessary, in order to discover what in fact caused the growth of eight churches in prewar Japan.

Two elements within Japanese social structure appear to have worked as dominant forces which nurtured the communal principle and hindered the substantial growth of individualization throughout the period of this study: (1) the tight family system; (2) the rigid hamlet structure. These forces acted both positively and negatively upon church growth but in the main they were largely responsible for frustrating the growth process. The importance of comprehending these systems of social structure is obvious and their "ideal types" (in the Weberian sense) as found in prewar Japan will be discussed in the following pages.

1. The tight family system. Many features of the "ideal" family system (and those of the hamlet structure) may be gleaned from the social system as it existed towards the end of the Tokugawa period (1600-1867). By then, the highly regimented and stratified society was made complete with the tight family system as its basic social unit. What were some of those characteristics?

One of the first to be mentioned was its economic aspect. Nearly eighty percent of Japan's total population at the beginning of the modern period (1868) lived in the rural area[5] and was engaged in agriculture with labor supplied by family members. With the scale of farming so small and poverty so great, the majority of the farming population in Japan was permanently reduced to a minimal living standard. In order to exist, the whole family — young and old, male and female — contributed their labor towards the family business. The need of the family took precedence over that of the individual; the family, not its constituent member, became solidified as a unit of activity and concern.

A second characteristic was the *ie* (house) ideology. The family as an *ie*, according to Fukutake, indicated the "continuing entity, perpetuated, in principle by patrilineal descent, from ancestors to descendants, an entity of which the family group at any one time is only the current concrete manifestation."[6] At some point in history, the family as an *ie* became further institutionalized even to the extent that the concept of *ie* overshadowed the family *per se*.[7] What this meant is made clear in the following:

> The distinguishing feature of the Japanese family system is the importance of the house as contrasted with an indeterminate group of blood relations loosely described as a family . . . To be more precise, the House is composed of the head of the House and of members who are subject to his authority. Those members may include not only his kindred by relationship of blood, but also persons, who enter the House with his consent. The House is in fact a name group and not a blood group.[8]

Several cultural symbols[9] have emerged for the purpose of ensuring the continuity of the house. Japanese culture has revered the close bond between parent and child. The members of each family were exhorted to conform to the "ways of the family" (*kafuu*). The physical house, family occupation, family property, family constitution, and family altar were handed down from one generation to another. These served functionally as visible symbols of family continuity and helped remind the individual of his belonging to the family-collectivity. What he did as an individual did count in that he either honored or dishonored his "family name" the entity of which included those living and dead and those yet to come. And thus it was by the frequent use of the words and expressions representing these cultural symbols that the person in the family hierarchy could easily implant, nurture, and strengthen the *ie* ideology in the minds of the rest of his family. The consequent result was to place a high premium on the importance of the group rather than on that of the individual.

A third characteristic of the Japanese family system was the patriarchal authority entrusted to the head of the house. Such absolute authority as to direct the entire family affairs was granted to him by consent of the society, legal or otherwise, because through it he was to superintend the continuity of the house. As a guardian of the *ie* ideology functionally imposed on him for his unique position, the head of the house could exercise his power even to expel the dysfunctioning member of the family from his family tie. This practice was called "kandoo".

The mistress of the household possessed limited power to oversee the domestic affairs. She managed the family finance; she was to see to it that the amount of money allotted by the head of the house stretched until the designated time of the month. Big items of consumption had to be approved by him before the purchase was made. Though she reared children and commanded their respect, the head of the house remained the final disciplinarian. It may be said that she exercised her largest influence upon the bride of her son. It was the solemn duty of the mother-in-law to train her daughter-in-law in the "ways of the family." In prewar Japan, the marriage could be dissolved by the head of the house for the reason that his daughter-in-law did not "fit into the family ways." The complexity of the family affairs paralleled to the complexity of the family structure in rural Japan. The bride was destined to bear the brunt of the whole system, but with patience and toil the day would come for her to be mistress of the household, if she was the wife to the heir. Then, the game of musical chairs turned in her favor. The young bride became the established member of the house. But until that day, she was to endure all things patiently. Soon the mother-in-law's power would dwindle as she grew older or when her husband died and her son (usually the eldest one) became heir to the headship of the household.

Under this *ie* system, the eldest son as an heir presumptive was naturally accorded a high status in the family. Unless he did something to destroy the confidence of his father, he generally succeeded to the headship of the house with all the privileges, rights, and obligations pertaining to it. The parents treated their eldest son with due respect, and their attitude towards him was clearly distinct from that towards their younger sons. Why this was so is explained below:

> There is no reason to believe that the intrinsic appeal of children to their parents depends on the order of their birth; it was, rather, a categorical imperative of the *ie* system that the heir should be given a higher status than his younger brothers. This was not only because he was destined to take on the headship of the family, but also because it was he who would have the responsibility of caring for his parents when they were old and helpless.[10]

Throughout the Tokugawa period, Japanese population was static at around thirty million. The problem of younger sons, therefore, was limited because many of them could inherit the wealth of other families by being adopted into a childless family or by becoming a *muko yoshi* (adopted husband) to a family with no son but a daughter to succeed the house. With the rise in population after the Meiji Restoration (1868), the problem of younger sons took on great sociological implications.[11] As Japan's industrialization progressed, it was largely from this reservoir of manpower that various industries tapped their labor force. This "event" of history, not to anticipate our future discourse, contributed greatly to the restructuring of Japanese society. At the present, it suffices to say that younger sons were placed subordinately to the eldest in the family hierarchy.

In a patrilineal society like that of prewar Japan, women were subservient to men and the birth of a daughter was no particular cause for joy to her parents. She would eventually leave the house and become a member of another family. Whatever investment was poured into her upbringing, plus her dowry, would be lost at the time of marriage, while younger sons, even after their marriages, could be counted on for help in a financial crisis at home. In fact, some younger sons, established in branch families, shared expenses to care for their parents with the eldest who now constituted the head of the stem (or main) family.

This prolonged discussion on the authority of the head of the house over the rest of the household has brought out an important fact concerning personal relations within the family: everyone had to act according to the prescribed code of behavior depending on his "station" in life. He learned the meaning of obedience and forbearance and the importance of accepting the *status quo*.

A fourth characteristic of the Japanese family system was the role which traditional religions played in reinforcing the family system. Shinto, Buddhism, and Confucianism each had a hand in tightening and preserving family solidarity and to the extent this was so, the process of individualization was retarded.

Shinto, as one writer defined it, is the "Japanese cult of a primitive animism with ancestral worship."[12] This was true of the household Shinto, and Shinto along with Buddhism and Confucianism supported the concept of family continuity by giving due reverence to ancestors. The family was firmly held together under common ancestry. Buddhism stressed the relativity of an individual and his life through the doctrine of *nirvana* which meant the "losing of self [or ego] in infinity."[13] The sacrifice of an individual for the sake of the family-collectivity became a culturally venerated virtue. Confucianism with its doctrine of "five relationships" accentuated concrete personal relationships "between ruler and ruled, husband and wife, father and son, elder brother and younger brother, and friend and friend."[14] In the Tokugawa period, at the height of feudalism in Japan, personal ethics were largely expressed in specific obligations "to feudal lord, to parents, to family, and, perhaps most important of all, to oneself, in the sense that one must properly play the role assigned to one by fate in a society of hereditary status."[15] Family solidarity (and the peace and stability of feudal society in the larger context) was achieved by binding its constituent members in the complicated network of obligations and by emphasizing loyalty and filial piety within the prescribed relationships. From the preceding discussion, little can we doubt the heavy role which traditional religions played in reinforcing the tight family system.

The "ideal" picture of the family system thus portrayed applied, except for minor differences, to all Japanese families of the Tokugawa period across class distinctions[16] and beyond geographical regions, though it may be pointed out that "it was particularly deep-rooted in farm families."[17]

2. The rigid hamlet structure. The individual in a farm family of pre-modern Japan was rigorously subjected to another kind of regimentation. He was first a member of his family, but at the same time he belonged to a larger concentric circle of hamlet community vis-à-vis his household.[18] The hamlet structure, like the family system, bound the individual in fetters and prevented the growth of individualization throughout the period of this study, but unlike the family system, its influence was confined to rural Japan. It may be said, therefore, that the individual in rural Japan was slavishly chained to the shackle of the tight family system compounded by the rigid hamlet structure. The family system having been elaborated, the task at hand appears to be to explain how the hamlet structure imposed its own pattern of thinking and mode of behavior upon the individual.

Johnson "ideally" describes the communal ethos of the Tokugawa hamlet as follows:

> It would seem safe . . . to suggest that generally the Tokugawa hamlet was a self-sufficient unit of social cooperation. Individual families carried out most activities needed for survival, and what they did not do was largely handled by the hamlet. It was the community, the *gemeinde*, consisting of contiguous households which considered itself a social whole.[19]

In other words, the hamlet was a closed, self-contained settlement composed of a number of households within relative geographical proximity to each other banded together for the purpose of cooperation. The very nature of agricultural production in Japan drew the hamlet members together as a working group. The predominance of irrigated rice agriculture necessitated the farmers to regulate the water supply among themselves. The hamlet collectively owned some uplands to grow grass for green fertilizers and to produce the material for roofing and building farm houses. Divided into several functional *kumi* (groups), the hamlet community acted in concert building a house, thatching a roof, constructing a road, maintaining an irrigation system, and doing any other work that was beyond the scope of single family labor.[20] Without the help of collective labor and benefits from common property, no average farm family could exist alone. "Hamlets," says Fukutake, "symbolized this unity in their protecting deity — the *ujigami* — and a shrine was a feature of every hamlet."[21] Thus, hamlet solidarity was based not only on economic foundations but also on a religio-spiritual heritage having the ancestral deities of the hamlet as common denominators. In similar vein, the hamlet cemetery served a functional purpose of uniting the community residents with their forebears. Nothing was more effective to rural Japanese than the appeal of common ancestry to cement the hamlet-collectivity. All other relationships being as they were, social life in the hamlet also took on a communal character. The process of socialization was often carried on in a peer group. A young man, for example, generally belonged to some sort of a youth organization in the hamlet. There he spent most of his leisure time. There he became more deeply oriented into group life; group acceptance was what he wanted. There he quickly acquired the skill to adjust himself to group norms by learning to echo the thought of his peer group as though it were his own. At every turn, from cradle to grave, the individual in rural Japan was too painfully reminded of his belonging to the collectivity which emphasized the dominant values of cooperation and conformity. No deviant behavior could be tolerated which threatened the "social whole" of the hamlet community. Should the individual dare commit a crime of noncooperation or nonconformity, various economic and social sanctions were sure to be given the deviator either individually or collectively with his family.

One possible economic sanction, apparent from our preceding discusssion, would be to cut off the water supply, grass, or firewood[22] from the household of the deviator. The water supply was the life blood to the farmer engaged in irrigated rice cultivation. Until the commercial fertilizing system was developed, grass and animal manure were the main sources of fertilization. Without access to the grass grown on common grasslands of the hamlet, no farmer could continue his farming. Money economy was slow to develop in rural Japan; therefore the daily need of firewood had to be supplied from the communal stockpile. The threat that his household might be cut off from these supplies of absolute necessity was a good enough reason for anyone to conform to the mores of the hamlet.

Another possible form of economic sanction might be subtle or overt pressure imposed upon the house of a lesser status by the house in a higher status. The traditional status of the family and its economic strength generally went hand in hand. Tahara speaks of "two dominant traditional types of social relations" in the hamlet as being those "between 'main family' and 'branch family', and those between landlord and tenant."[23] The main family held a high status and often possessed the economic power to sustain the livelihood of branch families at the time of their need. The main family was in many cases the landlord at the same time so that the economic relationship between landlord and tenant resembled the main-family-branch-family relationship. All the community relations, therefore, tended to take on a paternalistic character with the main family (or the landlord) ready to help the branch family (or the tenant) and conversely with the family of lesser status always ready to serve that of superior status. The landlords and the main families constituted the ruling few in the hamlet power structure. Thus, it may be stated that "the strength of community restraints was greater the lower one moved down the social scale. The independent individuality of those at the bottom of the hierarchy was wholly submerged in the community-like hamlet."[24] It is conceivable that few among the families of lower status dared to deviate from community expectations for fear of economic sanctions.

The intimate, face-to-face relationship of the hamlet community made social sanctions of various types a most effective measure of control. Ridicule was one form of social sanction often applied, especially among young people, to coerce the nonconformist to observe the accepted pattern of behavior. For example, "as soon as *buraku* people get wind of a [love] affair, they laugh at the principals."[25] The young man involved in the affair could very well be subjected to ridicule and avoidance at a youth gathering.

Another form of less stringent social sanction was gossip. It nevertheless conveyed the hamlet's disapproval of the undesirable conduct of the offender. Says Smith:

> Should a household fail to provide an adequate feast for those attending a wedding of one of its members, tongues will wag. If the daughter of a household is thought too free with her affections, word will get back to her family very quickly. Were a man to build what others consider an overly pretentious house, people will comment on his lack of judgment and label him a fool. Should a man prove always contentious in meetings of the hamlet association, there are many indirect ways to let him know that he is going too far.[26]

The sanction of noncooperation might sometimes be utilized to punish the violator of community norms.[27] It was customary for the hamlet members to help each other at various social and festive occasions. The rehabilitation of the offender could soon be accomplished through the inconvenience of noncooperation.

Occasionally, there were cases to which the ultimate sanction of *mura hachibu* (village outcaste) was applied. This was the most severe social sanction which the hamlet could give a household for the crime committed by one of its members. This generally meant the virtual cutting off of all ties with the hamlet community. The two offenses against the community which most likely would bring about ostracism are said to be: (1) "exposing the community to a public loss of face" and (2) "disturbing the peace and harmony of the hamlet."[28] One action liable to cause the second of the two offenses was "failing to maintain an established obligation with other hamlet households," and this included, among others, failure to participate in shrine festivals.[29] This is an important point and will be recalled later.

We have now completed our attempt to show (1) that the individual in rural Japan lived in a communal ethos of the tight family system compounded by the rigid hamlet structure and (2) that the violator of the "social whole" of the hamlet, either individually or collectively as a family, was subjected to various economic and social sanctions.

3. Regions in Japan. Before we leave the discussion of the Japanese social structure, a mention must be made of the existence of two major geographical regions, urban and rural, and their interaction in the context of history.

Urbanization is no exclusive legacy of industrialization, though undoubtedly its pace will be greatly accelerated by rapid industrialization of a nation. In Japan, there were already cities of various sizes at the beginning of the nineteenth century before the time of Japan's rapid industrialization. Edo (now Tokyo) and Osaka were highly populated, either having reached or nearing the population of a million.[30] The reason why Edo was then already Japan's largest city may be explained, according to Reischauer, by the "high degree of political centralization which underlay the feudal façade."[31] The Tokugawa clan with its victory over the Battle of Sekigahara (1600) established the hegemony of the Shogunate which lasted till the Meiji Restoration (1868). The clan ruled one-quarter of the country with the rest divided into two groups of feudal lords: (1) the *in-group* made up of eighty-six families who sided with the Tokugawa forces at Sekigahara and (2) the *outside clans* composed of one hundred and seventy-six families who took the opposite side.The officials of the Tokugawa regime came exclusively from the *in-group*. The strongholds of the *outside clans* were Choshu, Satsuma, Tosa, and Hizen all of which were located in southern Japan away from the capital of Edo.[32] The Shogunate in an effort to control the *outside clans* placed many restrictions on them, not the least of which was the system of *sankin kotai*. Under this system, feudal lords of the *outside clans* had to spend half of their time in Edo and their families were to remain there permanently as hostages of the Shogunate. The cost of frequent travel proved strenuous to the lords of anti-establishment, but they continued to be a viable threat to the regime and eventually, with help from the court nobles (*kuge*), overthrew the Shogunate at the Meiji Restoration. At any rate, travel of this kind opened up many trade centers along the main stretch on the Japanese archipelago. Osaka, for example, became the most powerful trade center in Japan where the feudal lords sold the products of their fiefs for money which they used in order to purchase rice for their stay in Edo.

Though by far the largest, Edo and Osaka were not the only cities. Kyoto, the ancient capital of Japan, remained a city specializing in fine handicrafts. Other cities developed around the castle headquarters of the feudal lords. The medium sized cities of Japan today are of this origin.[33] Describing the geographical concentration of the cities of present-day Japan, Reischauer writes:

> All her great cities and the vast bulk of her industries lie in a narrow coastal strip on the southern shores of Honshu from Tokyo to the tip of the island and then continuing along the north coast of Kyushu. If you draw a straight line from Tokyo 540 miles down the Inland Sea to the northwestern tip of Kyushu, you will find that within forty miles of this line and either on the sea or close to it are located thirty-three of Japan's forty-seven largest cities and more than half of her cities of medium size.[34]

Aside from the consideration of the accessibility to cheap maritime transportation and major sources of power, one definite reason for this unusual pattern of urban and industrial concentration was due to the heavy density of population in pre-modern Japan along the confines of this narrow belt.[35] Various classes of people lived in big cities like Edo and Osaka and in small castle towns of the Tokugawa period. There the *samurai* (warriors), artisans, and merchants — three of the four classes of people — made their abode. The fourth class, the farmers, came between the *samurai* and the artisans in the Tokugawa social stratification not because of their status but because of their usefulness to the ruling class. In fact, should the Japanese population of the Tokugawa period be divided into the classes and the masses, only the *samurai* class with levels of hierarchy within itself belonged to the classes and the rest the masses. The differentiation of these classes was due to the status ascribed by the feudal, hereditary system and not by economic achievement.

Outside these pockets of population density in the urban region, Japan before modern times was predominantly rural with people grouped in hamlets scattered over isolated areas of the land. We have already discussed the life in the hamlet. Here we examine the interaction between the city and the country by dealing with the "regions within a region." Japan's rural region, according to Fukutake, may be divided into the developed and underdeveloped regions. He makes a distinction

> between those areas where agricultural productivity was already fairly high in late Tokugawa times and where the subsequent progress of industrialization was rapid, and those areas where productivity had always been lower and industrialization was slower.[36]

The life in the underdeveloped region may more typically resemble the "ideal" hamlet life portrayed earlier.

The degree of disintegration of a region (or a hamlet) may be surmised as having been in direct proportion to the intensity of its contact with the urban and industrial center. In the more developed region, such factors as increased agricultural productivity, development of capitalistic economy, geographic and social mobility all contributed towards lessening the stress and strain of the tight family system and the rigid hamlet structure. The more developed area of the rural region was one stage removed from the city and took on many of the urban characteristics. But, to what extent the disintegration of the rural region took place in prewar Japan is the question we must constantly keep in mind. The basic fact about Japan's urbanization is that it was a slow process. The UNESCO report stated that "in 1899, only about 9% of the entire population lived in cities larger that 50,000, but in 1920 this percentage was about 16%, and in 1940 it had grown to over 34%."[37] This may appear to conflict with our earlier statement saying "nearly eighty percent of Japan's total population at the beginning of the modern period (1868) lived in the rural area." The difference of percentage is no doubt due to the difference in the definition of the "city" or "urban." Sato must have counted as urban those cities with less than 50,000 people thus making the percentage of the urban population in 1868 much higher. Our point nevertheless stands correct; urbanization was a slow process in prewar Japan. This rural-urban distinction (roughly sixty percent rural in 1940), according to Bennett, would place prewar Japan "in the general demographic category of agrarian Asian nations."[38] Except for a few large cities and the highly developed rural areas immediately adjacent to them, restrictions of family and hamlet controlled most of Japan's population.

Ecclesiastical Setting

The first Christian mission began in Japan on August 15, 1549 when the Spanish Jesuit by the name of Francis Xavier reached Kagoshima on the island of Kyushu. Japanese Catholicism during the subsequent three centuries was characterized by a unique yet tragic history.[39] The so-called "Christian Century" (1549-1639) witnessed a notable growth of that faith with an estimated membership of 300,000 in 1614 and also a series of persecutions reducing the membership to half by the end of the century.[40] The reign of Nobunaga Oda ended with his assassination in 1582, and with him went the protection of Catholicism. His successor, Hideyoshi Toyotomi, followed Oda's policy for a while, but soon came to suspect that the rapidly growing faith might overtake the hearts of his people, and his people the affairs of the empire. In a sudden fit of anger, he ordered the execution of twenty-six Christians by crucifixion which took place in Nagasaki on February 5, 1597. This was merely a preview of what was to follow. His death at the Battle of Sekigahara ushered in the reign of Ieyasu Tokugawa who firmly laid the foundation for the long-lasting Tokugawa regime. His campaign to exterminate all Christians within his empire commenced with the promulgation of his edict of January 27, 1614. Adherence to Christianity was strictly prohibited. Spae, referring to the extent of persecution, records:

> From 1614 to 1639 up to three thousand Christians were executed or died from torture or privation. Some thirty-seven thousand were massacred at Shimabara in 1638.[41]

Severe persecutions drove the Christians beyond their endurance culminating in the Shimabara rebellion which occurred near Nagasaki. It was put down by government forces with the above consequence. The following inscription, said to be found on the ruins of the Shimabara castle, well indicates the determination of the persecutor:

> So long as the sun shall warm the earth let no Christian be so bold as to come to Japan; and let all know that if the King of Spain himself, or the Christians' God, or the great God of all violates this command, he shall pay for it with his head.[42]

After this tragic episode, Japan tightly closed its doors for more than two centuries during which time the Christians were systematically sought out and were imprisoned, tortured, or executed. However, Catholicism did survive by going underground — an amazing story in itself.

The peace and stability of the Tokugawa period was suddenly threatened by the arrival of the gunboats commanded by Commodore Perry of the United States Navy at Uraga Bay on July 8, 1853. During the ensuing years, Japan had to deal not only with the United States but also with the other major Western powers which desired diplomatic and commercial relations with her. The first American consul, Townsend Harris, succeeded in persuading Japan to sign the treaty of Amity and Commerce in July of 1858. It was ratified a year later.

1. Protestant beginnings. The year 1859 marked the beginnings of Protestant mission in Japan. It was the year in which the anti-Christian edict of 1614 was still in effect, and in fact, as late as 1868, the "public notice-boards were freshly re-posted."[43] The cry of "Expel the barbarians!" was heard everywhere. The entire nation remained suspicious of, and hostile towards, the foreigners, and yet those who dared to venture out on their missionary work were hopeful that the situation would soon change. During the Exploratory Period, the following of our eight churches sent their representatives.

One of the three Episcopal societies, which joined in 1887 as the *Nippon Seikokai* (Holy Catholic Church of Japan), was the first to dispatch its missionaries to Japan. J. Liggins and C. M. Williams of the China Mission of the Protestant Episcopal Church of the United States of America were transferred to Japan, the former arriving at Nagasaki on May 2, 1859 even "before the actual opening of the ports."[44] A decade later (1869), the work of the Church Missionary

Society (C.M.S.) was represented by the Reverend George Ensor and his wife. In 1873 we find the third member of the future *Nippon Seikokai* at work, namely, the Society for the Propagation of the Gospel (S.P.G.) from Great Britain. The chief centers of these societies till about 1883 were Osaka and Tokyo for the American Episcopal Church; Osaka, Nagasaki, and Hakodate for the C.M.S.; Tokyo and Kobe for the S.P.G.[45]

The second group of missionaries to arrive in Japan was those of the Presbyterian and Dutch Reformed Churches: J. C. Hepburn, M.D., of the Northern Presbyterian Church in October, 1859 and the "triumvirate" of the Reformed Church in America a month later — G. F. Verbeck, S. R. Brown, and D. B. Simmons.[46] The Woman's Union Missionary Society entered the field in 1871 and in the next several years so did the other Presbyterian churches: the United Presbyterian Church of Scotland (1874), the Cumberland Presbyterian Church (1877), and the Reformed Church in the United States (1879).

To accurately describe the major steps in the development of the so-called Presbyterian Church in Japan is not easy, and the writer wishes to acknowledge his indebtedness to Dr. James Cogswell,[47] historian of the Presbyterian mission in Japan.

On March 10, 1872, there came into being the organization of the *Nippon Kirisuto Kokai,* the first Protestant church in Japan. This was the result of a series of prayer meetings held in Yokohama. The membership consisted of two middle-aged persons previously baptized and of nine students baptized together on the day of founding.[48] Though organized largely by the influence of Drs. James Ballagh and S. R. Brown, the church was completely non-sectarian at first. During the next few years, three other churches were established as part of this same *Kokai* in Tokyo, in the province of Ueda, and in Nagasaki.[49]

From 1873, another organization called the *Choro Kokai* began. This was an organization composed of distinctly Presbyterian churches brought into being by the efforts of individual missionaries.

Failure of the First Missionary Convention held in 1872 to unite all missions working in Japan prompted the Presbyterian and Reformed missionaries to maintain an organic union of the churches rising out of their labors.[50] Beginning in 1876, an effort was made to combine these two organizations. First there was the formation of the "Council of the Three Missions" including the Presbyterian Church, U.S.A. (North), the Reformed Church in America, and the United Presbyterian Church of Scotland. The successful negotiations between the Council and the existing Japanese churches resulted in the birth of the *Nippon Kirisuto Itchi Kyokai* (United Church of Christ in Japan) in 1877. At that time, this denomination was made up of nine churches, four from the *Nippon Kirisuto Kokai* and five from the *Choro Kokai*. In the succeeding years, the Council changed its name to the "Council of the United Missions" and still later to "The Council of Missions (Presbyterian and Reformed) Cooperating with the Church of Christ in Japan."[51] Other Presbyterian bodies that began work before 1881 also joined the Council and added their cooperation: The Reformed Church in the United States in 1886, the Cumberland Presbyterian Church in 1889, and the Woman's Union Missionary Society in 1896.

The Northern Baptist Church also began its work early in Japan. One of the sailors aboard Perry's expeditionary fleet was one Jonathan Goble. His observation of the situation in Japan at that time convinced him that as soon as the gate was opened the missionary work should commence there. Goble and his wife arrived at Yokohama in 1860 representing the American Baptist Free Missionary Society as the pioneers of the Baptist work in Japan. Until they returned to America in 1870, the Gobles worked in Yokohama for ten years preaching and teaching, translating and distributing parts of the New Testament.[52] The work was transferred in 1872 to the American Baptist Missionary Union later known as the American Baptist Foreign Mission Society. The *Annual Report* of 1873, summarizing the work of the Free Missionary Society, stated as follows:

> There are no disciples there as the result of Mr. Goble's former residence in Yokohama, no chapels, and no residences for missionaries. The work the Union has undertaken is, in fact, the establishment of a new mission, on very interesting ground; the great benefit of the above-mentioned transfer being the unity of effort which is thereby secured.[53]

Thus, the Northern Baptist mission began in Japan in 1873 with Nathan Brown who was originally under the appointment of the Free Missionary Society, but its heritage extended as far back as 1860.

The next to enter Japan was the American Board of Commissioners for Foreign Missions in 1869. The fruit of their labor began to appear in the spring of 1874 with the founding of two churches, one in Kobe with eleven members and the other in Osaka with seven.[54] From the beginning, they demonstrated enthusiasm to evangelize the nation. As early as 1878 there was a home missionary society among the churches that later came to bear the name of *Kumiai Kyokai* (Associated Churches). The idea of self-support was also germane to these early churches. Daniel C. Greene, the first missionary of the American Board, was being somewhat prophetic when he made the following observation in January of 1874:

> Whatever may be right elsewhere, there ought to be no question about having the Japanese support their own pastors and build their own churches from almost the first, if not from the very first.[55]

History bears out that the Congregational and Presbyterian Churches excelled in the growth of self-supporting churches and in the progress towards financial independence from their foreign boards. The early churches were able to assume responsibility for governing their own church affairs. The missionaries of the American Board quickly sensed the sentiment of the people and deliberately pursued the policy of not tying the national churches to their apron-strings. The relationship between them was one of "mutual sympathy and cooperation," and neither was enslaved to the will of the other.[56] In their organizational aspect, both the Congregational and Presbyterian Churches chose the representative form of government. Thus, early in the history of the *Kumiai Kyokai*, the ideas of self-propagation, self-support, and self-government began to grow. And to a remarkable degree, the same ideas were successfully nurtured in the Presbyterian Church.

Two other missions, the Methodist Episcopal Church and the Methodist Church of Canada, belonging to the same denomination started their work in 1873. The churches founded by these boards merged with those of the Methodist Episcopal Church, South, which began its work in 1886, to form the Japan Methodist Church in 1907.

When the leaders met on August 8, 1873 for the first annual meeting in Yokohama, they "proposed to pre-empt for Methodism the three largest islands of the Japanese empire." To implement the plan, they utilized the old-fashioned circuit system dividing the territory into four parts: the Yokohama, Edo, Hakodate, and Nagasaki circuits.[57] This early plan patterned the geographical distribution of the Methodist bodies for the ensuing years. The Methodist Episcopal Church occupied the northern section of Japan stretching southwestward to Tokyo and Yokohama with some work in the western half of the Kyushu island. The Canadian Methodists centered their efforts in the middle territory of the main island. The Southern Methodists, upon entrance in 1886, found themselves working in the area around the basin of the Inland Sea between the Northern and Canadian Methodists.[58]

One Methodist characteristic deserves our mention; from the earliest period, the Methodist boards emphasized education. They aimed at building "in connection with each local church a school, in each central station a high school, in Tokyo a college."[59] This characteristic would have bearing in the course of Methodist history in Japan.

The above survey shows that five of our eight churches were already represented in Japan before the present period closed in 1881.

2. Facts of growth. From 1859 to 1872 was a period with practically no church growth. Restrictions imposed upon the missionaries, their inability to communicate with nationals in Japanese, and an edict against Christianity greatly hampered evangelism. Christianity was called the "evil sect." The entire current was against those who would subscribe to it. There is no denying that the Edict in force for more than two and a half centuries implanted in the hearts of the Japanese ignorance and prejudice towards Christianity. Consequently, around the time of the Restoration, Christianity was regarded by the upper class people as an evil sect manipulated by politically ambitious nations; by the middle class people as heresy; and by the lower class people as black magic.[60] Thus, Christianity to most Japanese was something to be avoided and feared.

By 1872, in all Japan the total number of converts was eleven (five in Nagasaki and six in Yokohama)[61] and of missionaries was twenty-eight.[62] But there had come about

> a most remarkable modification of temper among official and influential men towards the missionaries, which reminded one of a change of climate. Instead of hostility, suspicion, or contempt, there grew up a spirit of respect for the missionaries, and of inquiry concerning the truth which was so nobly adorned by their labors and character.[63]

After the Edict was removed from the notice-boards in 1873, the general climate increasingly favored Christian mission. Church membership grew slowly till 1881. In all of Japan, there were approximately 1,600 communicants in 1878, 3,000 in 1880,[64] and not more than 4,000 in 1881.[65]

At the end of 1873, the records concerning the missionary force (including wives) of five churches appeared as follows:Episcopal (18), Presbyterian (29), American Baptist (6), Congregational (20), and Methodist (14) with the total of eighty-seven. And these were distributed in Yokohama (33), Tokyo (16), Osaka (16), Kobe (12), Nagasaki (8), and Aomori Ken (2).[66] Year by year, the number of missionary reinforcements increased and each mission endeavored to build up the national ministry. In large cities and some rural districts, churches were gradually organized. But in all these efforts, the period under review must be considered exploratory. Evidence of substantial church growth appears in the next chapter.

Church Growth Interpretation

The communicant membership of "not more than 4,000" in 1881 constituted merely a fraction of Japan's total population which was about forty million at that time. It was a modest numerical growth, to say the least. Perhaps, it was the best the church could do in those days given the unfavorable conditions which existed on the sides of both the church and the society. A limited number of missionaries working in Japan for the first time and many of them for a short while were to begin their missionary work from scratch. There was no Protestant mission previous to their coming, only the tragic history of Japanese Catholicism. Various aspects of Japanese social structure did more harm than good for the growth of the church. Yet, as embryonic as it was, the Protestant movement made its beginning. The task before us is to interpret this growth, modest as it was. This section raises two questions pertinent to the analysis of this development so that we may see the preview of the structure of growth which lasted throughout the period studied in this book.

1. To whom did the gospel make its appeal? It made its appeal primarily to sons of the former *samurai*[67] and secondarily to the rural population.

As noted earlier, the first Protestant church in Japan was organized in Yokohama in 1872. Japan's new relationship to the world made this port city the center of Western civilization; it was the show-window of the West in Japan in those days. Students (mostly the young *shizoku*) desiring to take advantage of Western education flocked to the city to learn English from the foreigners. Merchants and businessmen also came to the city for trade. These enterprising students made their way to the English classes taught by missionaries. These classes, which met in the homes of the missionaries, were the beginnings of the later Christian schools. It was quite reasonable, then, that the first church was to emerge from among these students who had intimate relationships with the missionaries and that its membership was "made up entirely of *samurai*."[68] Yokohama, of course, was not the only treaty port. There were four others (Nagasaki, Kobe, Niigata, and Hakodate) and two foreign concessions areas in both Tokyo and Osaka. According to Kudo,[69] the pattern of the church at Yokohama was reproduced in other big cities such as Tokyo, Kobe, Osaka, and Kyoto with the young *shizoku* as major constituents. The church spread from these places to the interior, to the old castle towns (which were made prefectural seats after 1871) where people of similar backgrounds lived. The converts of the early churches in Yokohama and Kobe conducted evangelism in their home towns. Missionaries could make tours into the interior for scientific and educational purposes, and they utilized the occasions to share the Christian faith. However, such efforts by both nationals and missionaries produced only a small response. The growth of the church at this early period was largely confined to big cities where most of the missionaries made their homes and where they conducted their "schools." Ikado was not far off when he wrote:

> In the beginning of the Meiji Era, the samurai Christians were the majority of the church members. The most active of them were then studying in the mission schools, which were at that time the only means for higher education and the only way to enter the intellectual class of the new society . . . In the early stage of missionary activities, therefore, to be a Protestant did to some extent mean to be a mission school student.[70]

Though constituting the majority of church membership, these young *shizoku* were not the only ones within the church. Data are sadly lacking on the early period, but it is within reason to suggest that a small percentage of the membership was occupied by the relatives of these young converts and by the former masses. In the latter case, an appreciable response was found only among certain people within the rural society.

For ten years from about 1877, Protestantism found its heyday in rural districts,[71] but the flare of "receptivity" was both extremely limited and short-lived. Kudo divides the ten-year stretch into two periods.[72] The first period (1877-1881) saw the pioneering in rural evangelism from big cities to their adjacent rural areas. There was some notable progress in Chiba Prefecture. During the second period (1885-1887), Gumma and Okayama Prefectures were reported as having been most responsive. The depression in rural districts characterized the intervening years (1881-1885), and the growth of the rural church was retarded, but soon the improved economic situation temporarily helped the church regain its momentum. However, a word of caution is necessary. During this ten-year period, Japanese Protestantism was accorded a most favorable reception never again repeated; however the rural church constituency was very small in proportion to the number of Christians in big cities. Undoubtedly then, the flare of "growth" of the rural church was tiny and short-lived.

After about 1887, or certainly after 1890, the strength of the rural church began to dwindle. During the remaining years of this study, the rural church never recovered its popularity and became virtually squeezed out of the village society. There are many reasons for this phenomenon, and they will be discussed later.

In connection with our first question, we have stated that the gospel made its appeal primarily to the young *shizoku* and secondarily to certain people of the rural community. The next question logically follows the first.

2. Why were they, and not others, more readily disposed to accepting the gospel? No single factor is adequate for the explanation. In the case of the *shizoku* youth, we give the following reasons.

First, their ready acceptance was due to the disintegration of the *samurai* class. The modernization scheme of the new government after the Restoration was bold and many changes were made rapidly under the slogan, *Fukoku Kyohei* (Rich Nation, Strong Army), with the desire to attain national security. The old clan system was abolished in 1871, and soon the government initiated a conscription system replacing the *samurai*. They were deprived of all political, economic, and social privileges given them in the feudal society. Furthermore, relieved of the master-servant relationship to their feudal lords, they experienced, as one contemporary put it, the "feeling of emptiness" in their hearts.[73] The lot of pro-Tokugawa retainers was worse because, after the Restoration, the positions in the Meiji government were filled by those of *outside clans*. Consequently, the more ambitious persons of the anti-establishment came to port cities and found their new object of allegiance and loyalty in Christ. Sociologically, this phenomenon may be conceptualized in the theory of deprivation.[74]

Second, their ready acceptance hinged on the fact that they were the intellectuals of the day and their training prepared them for it. From childhood, they received rigorous training in the Chinese classics and Confucianism. They were then the largest literate class. Only they could read the Chinese version of the Bible even before the appearance of its Japanese counterpart. Many of them, especially from the Jitsugaku school, were open to the new faith. This unlike the Shushi school was a liberal one and taught the positive teachings of Confucius. It provided a link between Confucianism and Christianity. Danjo Ebina spoke of his conversion thus:

> What made me overcome the obstacle in entering into the Christian faith was that I had an insight from the Jitsugaku school, which . . . discussed the matter of heaven and the world in relation to one's conscience; that is, one can go on his way toward heaven and in the world in spite of the rejection of parents. In the Jitsugaku school we personalized "Heaven," calling it "Jyotei" (Heavenly Emperor), believing that he saw our souls and protected us. That's when we seemed to know Christianity; we believed that *Jyotei* in Confucianism and God in Christianity are the same thing.[75]

Third, their ready acceptance was caused by "their desire that Japan should become a nation among nations."[76] Some of those who came to the missionaries were mostly interested in improving their lot, but many among them were serious-minded patriots who desired to lift the level of Japan to that of Western powers. Realizing that at the core of superior Western civilization lay the Christian faith, they accepted the faith as their own with the belief that the reform of their nation had to begin in their own hearts and in those of their countrymen.

Fourth, their ready acceptance was the result of an influence exerted by the unblemished character and disciplined life of the missionary.[77] By far, the largest number of missionaries was from America and of Puritan tradition. The life of a Puritan had much in common with that of a man from the *samurai* background. Many who came into personal contact with the missionary were influenced by him and his faith.

Fifth, their ready acceptance owed to the fact that they were least bound by, and detached from, the traditional mores of Japanese society. A historian, referring to the situation in port cities in this early period, stated:

> There were in these cities a large number of young people in whom the spirit of adventure was strong. Though not altogether free from family influence, they were not so much under the control of the family system as those who stayed around the old home. They were more easy to reach.[78]

In other words, the young people (mostly students) living in big cities away from their homes were the most detached in all Japanese society and were freer than anyone else to accept the exotic religion.

What was the case of the rural population? Why did a few of them respond? There are actually good reasons why Christianity should not have spread to rural Japan. Various restrictions weighed heavily upon the individual and his individual self was hardly emancipated from the collectivity of family and hamlet to which he belonged. Should a member of a household profess the Christian faith, he was sure to be disciplined individually by the mechanisms of control within the family system and collectively with his family by socio-economic sanctions of the hamlet community. The Christian conscience came in direct conflict with hamlet authority in the matter of participating in a shrine festival. Often the ultimate sanction of *mura hachibu* was applied in order to preserve the "social whole" of the hamlet. A further hindrance was the fear created by the tragic history of Japanese Catholicism. And still further, Buddhism was strong among the farmers. Naturally, the majority of rural population remained untouched by Christianity. Despite these difficulties, some people did respond and we must ask why.

Professor Morioka of Tokyo Kyoiku University has been an astute student of the church in rural Japan. His comparative study of three rural churches[79] founded between 1878 and 1896 is worthy of note. Though based on limited samples, the profile of the rural church which it depicts goes beyond the scope of its samples. Add to this our other data and observations, we will have the following answers to our query.

First, the rural converts were a particular kind of people within the community. They were the landlords, men of repute, and small industrial manufacturers of bean-paste and soya sauce or of sericultural products. And they were among the "literate and those of at least the middle class (the self-employed farmers) who, in the nature of their occupations, tended to be like city dwellers."[80] Being somewhat of an elite class, they were generally aloof from socio-economic sanctions of the community. In other words, those most likely to respond to the gospel were the social and economic elite who, while living in the country, were progressive, city-minded, and open to new ideas.

These individuals, in turn, became the channels through which the gospel spread. In the case of Annaka Church in Gumma Prefecture, the expansion took place along the family and friendship lines.[81] In Shimamura, the church grew among relatives and dependents of the rural elite. Morioka reports:

> When the head of a family is baptised, there is a strong tendency for the members of his family to be baptised en bloc, and his servants also tend to adopt their master's religion. The branch household in Japan was largely dependent of the main household and was likely to follow its actions and attitudes even in the matter of conversion to Christianity.[82]

This, of course, is an example of social structure working positively for growth. While requiring much pastoral care and spiritual guidance, this pattern of growth had high potential for a powerful Christward movement. But this did not happen in Japan for various reasons. And "since the great majority stuck to traditional Buddhism, conversion [in rural Japan] must be classed as 'deviant behaviour.' "[83]

Second, the areas of rural receptivity were those of the "developed region," in Fukutake's terminology, "where agricultural productivity was already fairly high in late Tokugawa times and where the subsequent progress of industrialization was rapid."[84] In these areas, the city influence was more acutely felt and, towards the latter part of rural receptivity, the old civilization began to show some sign of disintegration at least in its economic structure. People, like small industrial manufacturers and their employees, were outside the economic control of the local community. Yet, the majority of the rural population could not be freed too easily from their old mores and remained untouched by the gospel.

Third, during the similar period of rural receptivity, there was a movement for peoples' rights. This was a reactionary movement triggered by the government policy of land taxes. In order to modernize the national industry, the government needed capital and found the source in the form of land taxes. Both the landlords and the peasants were hurt by this policy. The landlords thought that they could be heard only by establishing a representative form of government. The movement composed of "school teachers, village headmen, landlords and to a lesser extent, the farmers themselves" gradually gained its momentum and spread most in "Chiba, Gumma, and Shizuoka prefectures and in the vicinity of Tokyo." Both the landlords and the farmers understood the connection between Christianity and democratic ideas (especially, the ideas of the worth of an individual and of the equality of men). And it is said that they flocked to the meetings addressed by Christian nationals and missionaries.[85] What we must avoid here is the ready association between the growth of Peoples' Rights Movement and the growth of Christianity in rural Japan. The study of the causal relationship between the two remains much to be desired. However, we may safely conclude that the liberal influence of the movement was one definite primer facilitating rural receptivity.

The flare of growth gradually subsided soon after 1887 for many of the same reasons that limited the growth of Protestantism after 1889.[86] But more specifically, we must note the suppressive measures taken by the government[87] over the liberal tendencies which hardened inherent rural conservatism. The government successfully destroyed the alliance between the landlords and the farmers by favoring the former. Disappearance of many of the economic pillars of the church from the rural churches was caused by repeated depressions in the countryside, the closing down of European markets for sericultural products, and change in the scale of industry. In the meantime, the children of the landlords received higher education and remained in big cities constituting part of the emerging white-collar class.[88] The rural churches were left with older members, and thus the flare of growth waned as time elapsed.

Already in this early period, we see many features characterizing the structure of growth which persisted during the entire period of our study. The majority of the early converts were the young people (mostly students) living in big cities at the time of conversion. While there was a notable rural response, the converts were primarily the rural dwellers with city mentality. And while there were some exceptions, especially in the rural community, the general way into the church was one by one, and the typical church was composed of those individuals extracted from their familial contexts. Often they were the only Christians in their homes. Also Japanese Protestantism was a class movement[89] from the very beginning. Its major constituents were of the middle class made up of descendants of the former *samurai* and the rural elite. They, according to Katakozawa,[90] were no other than the intellectual classes of the day. These features made the Christian converts the most detached of all in Japanese society free to respond to the gospel.

By 1881, the differences of growth among five churches were already noticeable. The Presbyterian Church was by far the largest and then the Congregational and Methodist Churches followed. At this early stage, the churches which made the most contacts with the responsive sectors of society grew faster. This meant the churches whose missionaries were capable of communicating with nationals had an advantage and grew faster. The size and quality of national leadership also had decisive influence upon growth differentials. The three churches mentioned above were more successful in organizing the national ministry, "each deriving most of its leadership from one of the [Christian] Band":[91] the Yokohama Band (Presbyterian), the Kumamoto Band (Congregational), and the Hirosaki Band (Methodist). In the next period, the differences among the churches become more pronounced, and we shall be able to give a fuller account of their growth and its analysis.

CHAPTER II

Openness to the West, 1882-1889

Socio-Cultural Setting

In the history of Japan, one observes an interplay between Japan's extreme pro-Westernism and anti-Westernism, between affinity to westernization and fear of domination by the West resulting in the rejection of everything that contained the Western influence. One era of pro-Westernism, according to Passin,[1] hit Japan during the period of the 1860's and 1870's which was followed by the conservative reaction from the late 1880's to World War I. Actually, it may be more accurate to say that Japan's openness to the West began to appear in the 1870's, with the determination of the Restoration government to modernize the country, and reached its height in the 1880's. In this section, we shall describe the factors which created this openness, particularly in the 1880's, and further ask the question: what kind of people were most susceptible to Western influences? Our effort in this chapter is to confirm our notion: the more open a segment of society was to the West, the more responsive it was to the Christian faith, especially when Christianity was regarded as the foundation of Western civilization. The churches which grew faster during this period were those which, for various reasons, were more equipped to take advantage of this receptive mood.

1. Factors which created openness to the West. The decade following the Restoration saw many drastic and extensive reforms in rapid succession. The leadership of the new government was made up of many young progressives from among the former *samurai* who were eager to build a rich and strong nation to ensure national security. Japan's contact with the West so deeply impressed its leadership of the "superior material accomplishments of the Western world" that "the Japanese not only became more determined to modernize their country along Western lines, but they tended to adopt generally the tastes, interests, and trappings of Western culture."[2] This modernization from above, as it were, took some time before it matured and the mood of the nation turned enthusiastically towards the West. In the 1880's, however, pro-Westernism was at its height, particularly among the intellectual classes. This is not hard to understand. In implementing the design of modernization, the government needed a large number of trained personnel "for the expanded bureaucracy, for the industrial program, and for the modern national army."[3] Therefore, in 1870 the central government issued an order instructing local officials to send "the most capable students to Tokyo," and the most prominent of them were further given opportunities to study abroad. In 1871 a Department of Education was established. In June of 1872, the government founded a normal school for the training of elementary school teachers and in August decreed the Fundamental Code of Education.[4] An old educational system was abolished and a new one initiated; education was no longer an exclusive privilege of the ruling class but was made accessible to those who desired it and were able to pay for it. The number of students, however, remained relatively small though it was on the increase year by year. Students, taught in public schools, were introduced to the democratic concepts of individual worth, freedom, and representative government by the use of American Readers. The names and teaching of men such as Washington, Jefferson, and Lincoln were familiar to them. "Among the more advanced groups in Japan," says Iglehart,

> the French Third Republic of 1875, was an exciting event, as were the changes in the new nations coming to life in Europe. A humanistic patriotism based on the writings of Rousseau and on the Enlightenment philosophers captured the minds of intellectuals.[5]

So the "revolution" of the seventies along Western lines was one factor contributing to Japan's openness to the West in general and

the government's educational policy in particular. The aim of training manpower for a modern state resulted in an increase of intellectuals who proved to be most receptive to Western ideology.

A second factor which created openness to the West was the
transformation of the basic economy of the nation "from agriculture
to one that was *increasingly* industrial, commercial, and
city-dwelling."[6] The development of capitalistic economy in Japan
was slow until the Sino-Japanese War in 1894; many facets of
industry were modernized after that time.[7] Yet, slow though it was,
certain progress was obviously seen on the agrarian-industrial spectrum. More areas in the rural region came to take on industrial-
urban features. In comparison with the period of the 1870's, more
people in the 1880's were living in larger cities in the style of life
which allowed individuals greater freedom from restrictions of family and hamlet. Also, more people were uprooted and experienced
confusion of values in this period of transition so that noble features
of Western civilization received ready acceptance.

A third factor contributing to the receptive mood was relative
freedom from fear of domination by the West. It was with fear and
trembling that Japan opened its door to the West in 1859. In fact, the
people "expected the worst."[8] However, after almost thirty years,
nothing had happened that justified their fear. No invasion by the
West took place in the 1880's, and "even the new activities and
teachings of the Christians were not too offensive."[9] This latter fact,
of course, is an important one in helping create a general atmosphere favorable to the West because, as we recall, the atrocities
committed by the Shogunate against the Catholics resulted from its
political rather than religious concerns, the greatest of which was
the fear of domination by the West.

A fourth factor which turned Japan into an avid Western en-
thusiast was the pressure for treaty revision. One of the urgent tasks
facing the Meiji government was to revise the unequal treaties with
Western powers which it inherited from the Tokugawa regime. The
terms of the treaties resembled "those forced on China by Western
powers, such as extraterritoriality and foreign control of tariff
regulation."[10] Japan had no sovereign rights to try the foreigner for
his crime committed on its own soil. Neither did it possess the rights
of determining its own customs tariffs. Under the terms imposed
upon it, "Japan was not to charge more than 5% *ad valorem* on all

goods."[11] This was a major roadblock to Japan's modernization program because its revenue through land taxes was limited and Japan needed to build its capital by raising customs duties. To improve the plight of the nation, a series of attempts were made to negotiate with treaty powers. As early as 1871, the government sent Tomomi Iwakura to Europe and America as ambassador plenipotentiary. In 1877, Foreign Minister Terajima began negotiations with the United States to secure independent customs rights, and America's sympathetic response materialized in the signing of a treaty between the two nations in 1879. But, the provision attached to the treaty prohibited its ratification when other countries such as Britain, France, and Germany refused to follow suit.[12] So Japan's efforts towards treaty revision in the 1870's ended in failure. This made Japan all the more persistent in attaining the desired goal. In 1882, the government enacted the new criminal code only to receive foreign criticism for its inadequacy. Thus, Japan in the 1880's was preoccupied by the thought of acquiring revision of the unequal treaties; in every step of the way, it seemed to have moved on the assumption that "the adoption of Western ways would not only strengthen Japan but would help her to become an acceptable member of the society of nations."[13] Consequently, affinity to westernization filled the spirit of the day.

> Dancing halls were sponsored by the government; English theatricals were given in higher schools; there was talk of adopting English as the national language; inter-racial marriage was discussed; Christianity was advocated as the national religion because it was the faith of the west.[14]

Some high ranking officials of the government took the lead in adopting Western manners and customs, and many followed. At times, people were admonished to westernize their ways in the name of patriotism. Anything that came in the way of progress towards westernization was deemed unpatriotic. Certainly, Japan in this period was keenly West-minded and demonstrated its enthusiasm by accepting things Western.

2. Kinds of people most open to the West. No doubt, some of the cultural and technological benefits of Western civilization rendered service to a greater part of Japan and the spirit of unbridled pro-Westernism permeated the larger populace. But it must be stated that only a comparatively small segment of the total population was

in a position to comprehend the phenomenon of westernization and take hold of the concepts of individual rights, freedom, and the democratic form of government. It is a considered judgment of one author who, speaking of the peasantry, wrote thus:

> This group had scarcely had time to understand what was happening to their nation . . . let alone had the opportunity to gain a perspective which would have made it possible for them to throw off the shackles of traditional Confucian authoritarianism.[15]

The peasantry of which he spoke constituted the "great underlying strata within the nation" in the 1880's. They were the victims of repeated depressions and inflation and at their sacrifices Japan was able to carry out its modernization scheme. Despite what was going on elsewhere, Western ideology had scarcely penetrated into the stronghold of traditionalism, and the people of the countryside remained generally unaffected by "Western fever." "It was not difficult, therefore," continued the same author, "for the oligarchs after 1885 to impose ever more stringently upon the great mass of the people an attitude of mind that had never been radically questioned by them."[16]

Who, then, were the kind of people most receptive to Western influences?

In earlier pages, we have already intimated several characteristics of the kind of people most open to the West. They were intellectuals, students (emerging intellectuals), urbanites or at least those living in more developed areas of the rural region, and some high ranking government officials. Among the so-called intellectuals were those who, by education, ability, and sometimes family status, reached the upper and middle class bracket within the Japanese society. If we combine all these features to come up with the ideal type of the people most susceptible to Western influences, then we must name those who, in the 1880's, came under the category of urban upper-and-middle class intellectuals and their protégés.

The upper class was largely made up of the members of the ruling oligarchy who were by no means "men of excessive wealth but they were inextricably related to those who continued to hold great economic wealth, the landed nobility, and the new financiers."[17] Between this small ruling class and the large peasantry was a middle class, the growth of which was hindered by the special character of economic expansion during the first two decades of the Meiji period.[18] Since Japan's economic development was initiated by the government with its heavy capital investment, there occurred no significant economic gain arising from private enterprises. Therefore, the development of a large middle class did not parallel Japan's economic growth. Even in 1889, "there would not have been more than a quarter of a million people in all of the professions"[19] making up the middle class. With gradual progress in modernization and industrialization, the period of the 1880's witnessed more specialization of economic activity with the consequent result of occupational diversification. Now, the middle class was composed of smaller landlords, some of whom were engaged in various village and household industries, descendants of the former *samurai,* some of whom became educators in the new school system and others of whom were managing petty commercial concerns or employed in large ones; and an increasing number of technicians and professional people who were needed to take on the responsibilities of a modern state.[20] Students above the primary grades were potential candidates to enter, if not already part of it, the privileged class either in its upper or lower bracket. That education during this period was still a commodity to be cherished only by children of the more well-to-do people may be seen from the government statistics of students belonging to this category: 22,000 in 1882, 26,000 in 1885, and 30,000 in 1889.[21] Thus, the kind of people most open to the West were limited to upper-and-middle class intellectuals in urban districts and their successors.

Ecclesiastical Setting

The period under review is an exciting one to study not only in terms of the panoramic history created by Japan's infatuation and courtship with the West, but also in terms of the growth of Protestantism from an embryo to a substantial movement. Adjectives such as "rapid" and "phenomenal" are often used to describe this growth and the year 1883 is commonly designated as its beginning, "though there is no one point that specifically marks the beginning of this period."[22] Our graph of growth (Figure 1, p. 6), however, indicates some upward trends from 1882. The reason for using the year 1883 is purely due to convenience in utilizing ecclesiastical landmarks and is not based on facts of growth. Cary, referring to this matter, recorded as follows:

This is partly because it was the year when important conventions
were held, and partly because it saw the beginning of a series of
revivals that exerted a powerful influence upon the Christians, and
through them upon unbelievers.[23]

The Second Conference of the Protestant Missionaries of Japan was
held in Osaka in April of 1883 and the Third General Meeting of
Japanese Christians in Tokyo a month later. And a series of revivals
followed. These events will receive our comments in due course.
Here we shall confine our endeavor to the laying of the ecclesiastical setting for church growth by introducing newcomers to the
field and presenting facts of growth.

1. Three new arrivals. The Disciples of Christ mission sent its first
missionaries to Japan in 1883 under the auspices of the Foreign
Christian Missionary Society (F.C.M.S.), the name of which was
changed in 1919 to the United Christian Missionary Society when it
merged with two other Disciples-related missionary societies and
numerous home agencies. The decision to open a mission in Japan
was made at the national convention of the F.C.M.S. in 1881.
George T. Smith and Captain Charles Elias Garst, a West Point
graduate, along with their wives were appointed as missionaries
and sailed from San Francisco on September 27, 1883, arriving in
Yokohama on October 19.[24] For several months, they spent much
time and energy learning the language, acquainting themselves
with the customs, surveying the field, and consulting with missionaries of other boards concerning the possible place to begin
their work. After much deliberation, they chose Akita, "a town of
40,000, situated on the west side of the main island . . . some four
hundred miles north from Yokohama."[25] Since in those days there
was no train to take them to Akita, they went by sea. There the
American Baptists and the Disciples worked closely in evangelizing
the northern part of the island. Preaching, conducting Bible classes,
visiting homes, and selling Bibles and tracts characterized their
work. Until 1900, the Disciples strictly followed the policy of direct
evangelism. On July 30, 1884, after about two months in Akita, the
mission received its first convert from a non-Christian faith and in
1887 organized its first church. Akita remained as the only station
occupied by the Disciples during this period.

The Presbyterian Church in the United States, more specifically
the Southern Presbyterian Church, was the second to arrive. Faced
with Japan's unusual openness to the West and to Christianity,

missionaries of various denominations were requesting reinforcements from home. One such request was made by Dr. James H.
Ballagh of the Reformed mission in early 1885 in a letter to the
Executive Committee of Foreign Missions of the Southern Presbyterian Church. "We feel," wrote Ballagh,

> that the harvest is already on us, and the laborers are far too few. Our
> Reformed Church cannot increase her force . . . So we must look to
> our brethren of the Presbyterian family to come to our rescue.[26]

With an offer of a memorial gift from the Grand Avenue Presbyterian
Church of St. Louis honoring its deceased pastor, the plan of begin-
ning missionary work in Japan was discussed by the Executive
Committee and approved by the General Assembly. Soon Randolph
Bryan Grinnan and Robert Eugenius McAlpine were on their way to
Japan.

On December 3, 1885, only two days after their arrival in Japan,
the Presbyterian Council of Missions at its meeting in Tokyo heartily
welcomed the newcomers as co-laborers. Before these young missionaries were laid three cities from which to choose their place of
missionary endeavor: Sendai, Nagoya, and Kochi.[27] The Council
felt that perhaps the northeastern city of Sendai might be more
appropriately served by the people of the German Reformed Mission who were accustomed to severe wintry weather. After visiting
Nagoya and Kochi, Grinnan and McAlpine decided on the latter
city which was more open to missionary work, the former city being
one of the fortresses of Buddhism. Kochi's receptivity of Christianity
was largely due to the influence of one man, Taisuke Itagaki. A
native of Kochi (the former Tosa[28] province), he founded Japan's
Liberal Party, an ally of the Peoples' Rights Movement. Thus, it may
be said that Kochi was "one of those rare places in Japan where new
ideas, whether in the political or the religious sphere, found a ready
welcome."[29] More concretely, Itagaki openly commended the acceptance of Christianity to the people of his province, when he
learned that the change in the moral fiber of some of his friends was
caused by their becoming Christians. He reasoned that "his liberal
political program needed a moral strength that none of the native
religions offered," though he himself never became a Christian.[30] A
group of missionaries including Dr. Verbeck responded to the invi-
tation issued by Itagaki and made a visit to Kochi in 1884 to discover
a great enthusiasm towards Christianity. As a result, a church was
born in Kochi on May 17, 1885 with twenty-two members even

before the Southern Presbyterian brethren arrived there. The church grew until it had the membership of 625 in 1890.[31]

The pioneer missionaries were joined by others and by 1888 the number reached fourteen. And with the coming of reinforcements, another station was opened in Nagoya in 1887.[32]

In the previous chapter, we have already referred to the beginning of Southern Methodism in 1886. The interest to begin missionary work in Japan loomed high among the Methodist Episcopal Church, South, as early as 1860 as evidenced by the appointment of W.J. Sullivan as a missionary. Unfortunately, the Civil War interrupted the project. Two and a half decades elapsed before the matter was again taken up by the church. Following the resolution of 1885, the Board of Missions appointed, in 1886, Dr. and Mrs. J.W. Lambuth, Dr. and Mrs. W.R. Lambuth, and Rev. and Mrs. O.A. Duke as their representatives who reached Kobe in July of the same year. These missionaries were working in China at the time of their appointments. Bishop A.W. Wilson formally organized the mission on September 17, 1886.[33]

Evangelism was stressed by the new mission as its basic policy and the statement read:"To hold on to the Methodist itinerancy and not suffer ourselves to get too much involved in educational work."[34] But the unique character of the responsive population in Japan dictated the mission to employ the educational method. Due largely to the efforts of the Lambuths, there came into being great educational institutions of Southern Methodism: the Kansei Gakuin (1889) and the Hiroshima Girls' School (1893).

The period between 1882 and 1889 thus saw one new beginning and two existing missions reinforced by their ecclesiastical relatives. Other churches, too, were joined by their new recruits. The Protestant movement during this period showed a remarkable success, and the historians of the church often look back on it nostalgically as the golden age for Protestantism. It is a misnomer to think, however, that all churches were favored by similar growth in this period. Facts of growth reveal different patterns and must precede their analyses.

2. Facts of growth. The growth patterns of various churches can be depicted only when facts of communicant membership (see Figure 1, p. 6) are clearly before us. The Wonderful Seven Years, 1883-1889, have been beautifully described by Dr. Winburn Thomas in *Protestant Beginnings in Japan,* but he has not given the

record of each denomination. It is essential to see the actual record of each church. In the period between 1882 and 1889, Congregational and Presbyterian Churches made extremely rapid gains, — the Congregational Church from 1,000 to 9,000, and the Presbyterian Church from 2,000 to slightly less than 9,000. The former multiplied by nine — increased over 900 per cent and the latter by 4.5 — 450 per cent — in less than ten years. The Methodist Church which was on equal footing with the Congregational Church in 1882 advanced in this period, but not as greatly. The Episcopal Church stood still till about 1887, and then gained consistently. The American Baptist Church and the Disciples of Christ made very slight progress. Only for the first two or three churches was this period the "golden age."

A further examination of Figure 1 (p. 6) informs us that growth in the latter half of the period was more rapid than that in the first. Later we shall explain this phenomenon.

The ripeness of the field does not guarantee a great harvest. Much depends upon the quality and quantity of laborers and the tools with which to work. By the same token, church growth does not occur without laborers and tools which together may be called the mission machine. Given the ripe field of the 1880's, some churches were able to grow faster provided that they possessed the right mission machine. Much concerning the growth of the church can be explained by scrutinizing the mission machines of various churches. We shall elaborate on the increases in missionaries, national forces, and churches in order that we may draw on these facts in the next section.

Table 1

Increases in the Number of Missionaries Including Wives, 1882-1888

Church	1882	1885	1888
Episcopal	48	48	75
Presbyterian	81	107	135
A. Baptist	13	18	29
Congregational	43	44	76
Methodist	40	53	77
Disciples		4a	8

a. The 1883 figure of four was used because the 1885 figure was unobtainable.

Source: Compiled from *Proceedings of the General Conference of Protestant Missionaries in Japan, Tokyo, October, 1900* (Tokyo: Methodist Publishing House, 1901), pp. 819, 988, 989. Hereafter referred to as *Tokyo Conference Report*.

From the above table, a few facts are clear. First, by 1882, all churches which began work before 1873 more than doubled their missionary forces. Second, the latter half of the period saw more reinforcements than the former in all churches. Third, churches which merged within the ecclesiastical family naturally had more missionaries than those working alone with the notable exception of the Congregational Church. Fourth, Congregational and Methodist Churches had an almost equal missionary strength during the entire period, though there was by 1889 a great difference between them in the growth rate of communicants.

No mission board could send an unlimited number of missionaries to the field. Therefore, the battles of church growth were inevitably won by the hands of able nationals. The following table indicates the growth of ordained national ministers and other helpers including unordained preachers, catechists, and Bible women (women evangelists who often assisted female missionaries). The latter figures fluctuate more readily, but nevertheless they serve as one useful indicator explaining church growth.

Table 2
Ordained Nationals and Other Helpers, 1882-1888

Church	1882		1885		1888	
	Ordained	Others	Ordained	Others	Ordained	Others
Episcopal	2	19	2	19	6	71
Presbyterian	28	18	32	26	43	55
A. Baptist	2	17	3	21	6	32
Congregational	13		19	22	27	44
Methodist	11	32	15	98	22	69
Disciples					1	1

Source: Compiled from *Tokyo Conference Report,* pp. 988, 989.

The Episcopalians and the Baptists, two of the earliest arrivals in Japan, were slow in nurturing their national leadership. After about thirty years of work, they were able to raise only half a dozen ordained ministers, though their helpers numbered considerably. The Presbyterian Church ordained the highest number of ministers. Even in the matter of ordained ministers, Congregational and Methodist Churches were close parallels to each other throughout this period. The Disciples being the newest arrival was, of course, the slowest.

Accompanying the growth of church membership, there was a gradual increase in the number of organized churches, some of

which were wholly self-supporting including their pastors' salaries.
Note Table 3 for the differences among the churches.

Table 3
Organized and Self-Supporting Churches, 1882-1888

Church	1882 Organized	1882 Self-Support	1885 Organized	1885 Self-Support	1888 Organized	1888 Self-Support
Episcopal	15	0	15	0	47	6
Presbyterian	37	1	45	4	61	18
A. Baptist	9	0	8	1	10	4
Congregational	18	13	28	13	43	40
Methodist	14	0	16	0	35	0
Disciples					1	0

Source: Compiled from Tokyo Conference Report, pp. 990-992.

Congregational and Presbyterian Churches greatly advanced in
creating self-supporting churches, the former by far out-numbering
the latter. Episcopal and Methodist Churches, on the other hand,
made little or no progress. All these denominations, however,
added a number of organized churches especially during the second half of the period. The Baptists and the Disciples were marked
by their slow development in organizing churches.

With external and internal conditions influencing the church
partly described as above, we shall now proceed to interpret the
phenomenon of rapid growth enjoyed by some churches and that of
slow growth achieved by others.

Church Growth Interpretation

Striking differences in the rate of growth among the churches can
be explained by not one but many factors. Church historians and
missionaries attempted various explanations to account for the
"phenomenal" growth of the 1880's, but no substantial work had
appeared before Thomas wrote his doctoral dissertation[35] at Yale
University in 1942. His work, therefore, merits careful study. In this
section, we shall first look to Thomas for his contribution and then to
other sources for supplemental factors in order to unravel the knotty
problem regarding the structure of growth which prevailed during
this period.

1. Findings by Thomas. Among many discoveries contained in
Thomas' work, we shall seek answers to two specific questions: one
concerning the strata of society among which Protestantism spread

most and the other related to the causes of rapid growth of some
churches over others during this period.

Our first question may be phrased thus: where and among what
classes of people did Protestantism spread most? Thomas, after
carefully examining available sources, concluded:

> Protestant Christianity spread . . . primarily in the urban population
> centers, and only secondarily in the rural areas; and its greatest
> strength was among the educated, upper middle classes of the
> population.[36]

For various reasons,[37] the church fortified its strength in the cities.
One of the obvious reasons, of course, was the concentration of
missionaries there. Without passports, missionaries were unable to
leave the treaty settlements. Even those who resided in the interior
made their homes in the cities where they were employed by the
Japanese as school teachers. Also, the fact that students and former
samurai were moving to the cities provided ample opportunities for
the missionaries to make contacts with the responsive sectors of
Japanese society without having to leave the settlements. Furthermore, the number of missionary teachers was far too small to staff
the existing mission schools so that little was required of the missionaries to go beyond the limits of the treaty regulations. Another
reason for the urban strength of Protestantism in Japan was that "the
largest number of converts, the students, remained in the cities
rather than returning to the provinces."[38] They remained in the cities
because urban areas afforded more job opportunities and were
intellectually more emancipated than rural districts. A third reason
was purely economic: "There was more money in the urban areas
to maintain an exotic religion."[39] The ideal of self-support being
high among the missionaries and nationals, efforts were made to
obtain that goal as rapidly as possible. Consequently, churches
were more readily organized in urban rather than rural districts.

Protestantism's "major success among the educated classes"
placed a stamp of intellectualism upon the church.[40] Students from
all over Japan — children of the rural elite, of national and prefectural officials, and of the wealthy merchants in the cities — flocked
to mission schools. And missionary educators were awaiting their
coming, since education was the dominant method of evangelism
available to them. The "mission schools" at this time were rudimen-
tary, however. Classes were held in the homes of missionaries at first
and were highly evangelistic. Students studied the Bible and mis-

sionaries prayed that their students might become Christians.
"Dormitory life, especially, was Christian in atmosphere."[41] The
mission schools during this period then were a far cry from those of
the 1930's or today. Also, the desire of the missionaries to raise an
educated church with a trained ministry dictated an emphasis on
education. Apparently, during the receptive period of the 1880's,
even those who crowded the churches in general were from the
intellectual classes. Anesaki's remark aptly suggests this when he
wrote that the crowds "listened to sermons delivered by missionaries — preferably in English."[42] The persons who had even a
smattering of English in those days were either students or their
equivalents who were rightly classified as intellectuals.

The urban and intellectual characteristics of church membership
are made clear, but how are we to interpret the fact that the majority
of them belonged to the upper middle level of the population?
According to Thomas,[43] the church with its desire for self-support
naturally worked with the class of people capable of paying for its
local expenses. Most converts through the mission schools either
were self-sufficient prior to their entrance or became so shortly after
their graduation. One additional factor destined the Japanese
church to take on the upper middle class character; thirty percent of
its constituency came from the *samurai* class, the ruling class in the
feudal society. The ratio of former *samurai* within the church membership was very high considering that they comprised only five
percent of the total population.

Our second question may now be put as follows: why did some
churches grow faster than others during this period? Thomas answers the question with three specific reasons, but others may also
be gleaned from the corpus of his writing.

First, "the most effective missions were . . . the strongest nu-
merically and financially."[44] It is obvious from Table 1 (p. 49) that
the fast growing churches on Figure 1 (p. 6) were more endowed
with foreign personnel than the bottom two. With the particular
conditions that encountered the early period of Japan mission, two
elements were crucial for church growth: the strength of the missionary force and the financial backing of productive programs such as
carrying on educational institutions.

Second, "the policies of the several missions relative to the concentration of forces likewise affected the growth of the churches
associated with them."[45] The Congregational Church concentrated

its missionary force in several key stations and grew fastest during this period, while the other missions had a much lesser degree of concentration. The Episcopal Church followed the policy of dispersion "casting the evangelistic net" widely across the nation, the fact of which, says Matsudaira, proved to be beneficial to its future development.[46] But, the widespread location of the missionaries at least in this period afforded the Episcopal Church much slower growth than others. Between these two poles lay the Presbyterians and the Methodists who, while recognizing the necessity of avoiding dispersion, were less concentrated than the Congregational Church in stationing their missionaries. To be sure, preference of the policy of concentration over that of dispersion is a tricky one and must be weighed carefully. The wisdom at work here is to prevent the churchly forces from scattering too thin to be effective. Furloughs and illnesses often deprive the stations of their missionary presence and their continuity. Yet, with the increase in the number of missionaries and especially of trained national forces, a good case can be made for favoring dispersion to secure more contacts and to plug one prominent source of membership leakage caused by geographical mobility. This matter will be referred to in later chapters. During this relatively early period, however, Thomas' point seems to stand correct.

Third, the rate of growth was influenced by "the kind of Japanese taken into the church and the extent to which administration was transferred to national leadership."[47] The Congregational Church was most successful in attracting the largest number of outstanding Japanese. Men like Niijima and Sawayama and the Kumamoto Band played a decisive role in bringing into the church others of their caliber. The Presbyterian Church with Masahisa Uemura as its key figure did not lag too far behind the Congregationalists in attracting and training able leaders. Furthermore, these two churches were more capable of gathering "men and women of ability" within their memberships who gave the Christian faith and their churches "nation-wide prestige, influence in official circles and validity among the student class."[48] It is interesting to note that the Baptists were unable to include within their rank a single outstanding leader or scholar among the Japanese.[49] Baptist missionaries were largely responsible for winning the converts and the pattern of missionary centered evangelism did not issue in great growth. On the matter of transferring administration to national leadership, it was also the Congregational Church which was most liberal and, in fact, the American Board reportedly had no policy concerning this point when the subject came up.[50] The more able the Japanese taken into the church were, the more independent and nationalistic they were, and the transfer of administration was more quickly transacted. Both Congregational and Presbyterian Churches were the earliest to achieve this status.

Fourth, the fast growing churches were "those with affiliated schools."[51] All churches besides the bottom two stressed education[52] during this period and were able to ride Japan's tremendous surge for knowledge. "Schools," writes Thomas, "were of primary importance in the policies and programs of the mission agencies and churches."[53] The Baptists and the Disciples followed the single line of direct evangelism and were slow catching on to the innate desire of the Japanese for education. Or, if they were aware of it, lack of missionary personnel and funds undoubtedly would have hindered them from establishing educational institutions.

Fifth, the spirit of self-support accelerated church growth. The first missionary of the American Board, D.C. Greene, came to Japan with a charge "to hold as his one great object the promotion of independent and self-supporting churches."[54] The policy of that church was inspirational to others. Especially among Congregational and Presbyterian Churches the spirit of self-support was high and the two denominations were more successful than any others in producing self-supporting churches (see Table 3, p. 51) by virtue of having most qualified national leaders and members of high social status who demonstrated their strong characteristics of independence and patriotism even in church affairs.

Sixth, the slow growth of the Episcopal Church was partly due to its liturgical form of worship, because there was "a reaction against ornate Buddhist ceremonies."[55] Such reaction was not universal but was keenly felt among the intellectual classes in urban districts. Ceremony was minimized in other churches because of "the strength of Congregational and Presbyterian simplicity among the missionaries."[56]

To sum up, Thomas' findings clearly indicate that the church membership during this period was mainly composed of urban upper middle class intellectuals with the largest number of converts from students. Moreover, given Japan's unusual openness to the West and its dominant religion, the churches which grew fastest were those which had most missionary personnel and finance; which attracted most able nationals within the ranks of their leadership; and which emphasized missionary concentration, education, self-support, and simplicity of worship.

2. Supplemental factors. Additional data enable us to illumine the anatomy of converts and to further explain the patterns of growth.

Professor Sugii's unpublished manuscript[57] contains important information concerning the persons baptized before 1890. Keiseisha, a publishing firm, undertook in 1917 a project of compiling brief biographical sketches of people with thirty years of Christian life. Names of qualified persons were submitted to the publisher by the local churches, and questionnaires were mailed to 2,500 such persons. The firm received 859 returns which were filled out either by these people personally or by their relatives and close friends in the case of the deceased. Using the project, published as a book in 1920, as the basis, the history professor at Doshisha University made a painstaking analysis. With the author's kind permission, we shall elaborate on the anatomy of converts before 1890.

First, we note the predominance of males among the converts. Out of 859 persons, there were 567 males and 292 females including six persons (three males and three females) who were baptized as infants.[58] A book published in 1891 confirms Sugii's data when it reported that "the membership of the Japanese Churches consists in large majority of males."[59] One of the reasons for the male dominance, says Sugii, was that young men had more opportunities to study Western education than young women. Most women who did become Christian were graduates of mission schools for girls.[60] Another reason was that the feudalistic family system bound young women more tightly than young men to the conservative, traditional mores and views of life.[61]

Second, we note the age distribution of the converts at the time of baptism. Forty percent of the respondents were baptized between the ages of sixteen and twenty-three. The percentage rose to sixty-seven when the persons between the ages of sixteen and thirty were tolled. The peak was eighteen years of age. According to Sugii, the fact that many young people accepted the Christian faith readily implies that the gospel was received in the process of acquiring Western education and culture.[62] Among the females, there were two peaks, one at the age of sixteen and the other at twenty. The first

peak coincided with the time of graduation from the girls' school
and the second with the period within two or three years after
marriage. Sugii understands this to be the influence of Christian
husbands upon their wives. It is said that a considerable number
were baptized on the same day as husband and wife, while others
were joined by their wives a few years after their marriage. These
two peaks were surrounded by deep valleys and Sugii alludes this
fact to the difficulty of women in a rigidly feudalistic society to make
a profession of faith contrary to that of their ancestors.[63] It is clear
from the age distribution of the converts that a large percentage of
them were baptized as students and others shortly after their graduation from the schools. Though missionaries and Christian scholars
teaching in government schools guided many to the Christian faith,
"perhaps by far the greatest number of converts," as Best wrote,
"came from the schools established by the missions of which there
were 101 of all kinds by 1889 touching yearly some 10,000
pupils."[64] Thus, the influence of mission schools in the spread of the
gospel is undisputable. Thomas was quite within reason when he
suggested that Protestantism in Japan had been "from the first a
student movement."[65]

Third, we note the motives of church members at the time of
baptism. From the descriptions given in the book as to their motives
of accepting the faith, Sugii classified the respondents into three
categories.[66] Type I consisted of those who became Christian while
studying Western education, by having been impressed with Christian teachings, by realizing the poverty of traditional religions upon
encountering the Christian faith, by observing good Christian examples in the lives of missionaries and national pastors, or by
adhering to the Christian claim that all men are created equal. This
type caused no radical discontinuity within the believer upon becoming a Christian. Sugii uses the term "chokunyu-gata" (the pattern of straight entrance). We may say that it was an intellectual way
into the faith. Here the Christian faith was conceived more as an
ethic than a religion and, if a religion, it was more as the religion of
the head; Christianity to most converts was something to be learned
as one studied the subject of American history or mathematics.
Inasmuch as Christianity in Type I was regarded as a learning, we
may call this intellectual way into the church the "school
approach."[67] The term is appropriate because the largest number of
converts came from the schools where students were either formally

instructed in the Bible or enrolled in extracurricular Bible classes for a period of time and then received baptism. The number would swell, if the "post-graduate converts"[68] were counted. Though there were evidences of people being baptized along with their loved ones as families notably among the rural converts, the dominant way into the church was nevertheless one by one "rather than mass conversion."[69] Knowing the communal pattern of religious response in Japan, the Protestant missionaries took pains to emphasize the need of personal repentance and individual salvation and were skeptical of conversions in large quantity as in groups and families. Also, their own response to the gospel was individualistic and they naturally expected the Japanese to respond in a similar fashion. The school approach then may be characterized by the intellectual and individualistic response to the Christian faith.

Type II was made up of those who entered the faith through shattered experiences of life such as unbearable loneliness by separation from loved ones, sufferings from interminable illnesses, or family tragedies. Sugii designates "kussetsu-gata" (the pattern of refraction) to this type. We may express it as an experiential way into the faith. The convert had radical religious experience. To him, Christianity was a matter of the heart and of deep emotional involvement. The greater his problem, the larger his joy of salvation. Given the intensity of such religious experience, he perhaps could not help but desire the salvation of his family, relatives, and friends. We wish to label this experiential and "group-oriented" way into the church the "conversion approach." Type III included people with both kinds of experience. The tabulation indicates that eighty-two percent of the total respondents belonged to Type I. "This simply means," says Sugii,

> that Christianity enjoyed favors brought about by the enthusiasm for Western learning, the popularity of Europeanization, the work of mission schools, the expansion of the educational system, and the imitation of superior culture.[70]

"This also means," continues the author, "that the people most responsive to the Christian faith were of the intellectual classes of the day."[71]

Our exposition of Sugii's data has given us overwhelming evidence that the major way into the church was through the mission schools during this period in the sense that the majority of church members were either student converts or post-graduate converts. In comparison with young women, young men were less bound to the traditional family system and were given more opportunities to study Western education. In fact, Protestantism pioneered in women's education which was totally neglected by the state. Thus, women were intellectually less emancipated than men and were slow to respond to the Christian faith. The predominance of males within the church membership readily proves the point. Furthermore, Sugii has done a great service to us by his analysis of the converts' motives. Based on his analysis, we were able to typecast two dominant "approaches" to the Christian faith. In Chapter V, we shall make use of these ideal types and draw a vivid contrast between them. The writer is firmly convinced that the school approach ("chokunyu-gata" in Sugii's terminology) dominated the Protestant world and the conversion approach was an exception in prewar Japan.

In discussing the patterns of growth, we shall give further reasons for the growth differentials among the churches and also take account of the post-1885 rapid development.

Referring to the growth pattern of the two largest churches, Gordon in 1892 wrote as follows:

> It is beyond question that their representative form of government has been a great aid to the evangelistic work of the Congregational and Presbyterian churches.[72]

How was this so? Perhaps, given the age in which a certain segment of society was yearning for representative government, the churches based on that democratic principle were able to draw people from that sector of society. Furthermore, the two denominations provided within their ecclesiastical systems opportunities for aspiring, able nationals to exercise their leadership. On the other hand, "the hierarchical polity of the Methodist and Episcopal churches, and the reluctance of the Baptist missionaries to concede authority handicapped these denominations."[73] This fact in itself is an indictment upon the quality of leaders taken into various churches. Certain church polities either brought out or discouraged the initiatives on the part of the nationals and affected church growth.

Now we shall make a few comments on the pattern of the slow growing churches. Though the Episcopal Church after 1887 made a steady and considerable growth, it should be classified along with the bottom two at least during this period. It is somewhat of a wonder to many persons why the church that began as early as 1859 and possessed as many missionaries as Congregational and Methodist Churches did progressed so slowly in building up its membership. Some answers are already given. We shall add another: the policy of Bishop Williams concerning thorough preparation. Writing the bishop's biography, Mutch stated:

> Williams believed in thorough preparation not only for his catechists, the lay workers, and candidates for Holy Orders, but even for those who desired baptism and confirmation . . . This tradition of from six months to two years preparatory instruction for converts and of as much as from six to ten years preparation for the priesthood has continued to the present.[74]

The slow growth of the Episcopal Church was caused by the prolonged waiting before baptism and by its inability to raise many able nationals in the rank of its leadership. What was necessary was not an unduly prolonged preparatory period but the training of the converts and the leaders as thoroughly and quickly as possible.

The slow growth of the American Baptists may be attributed to the fact that "the workers were changing often and reinforcements were few"[75] until 1889. Also, the Baptist Church kept its missionaries widely spread and the line was too thin. Furthermore, the Baptists followed the autonomy of the local church more strictly than the Congregationalists so that they were unable to maintain cohesiveness among their churches.[76]

The Disciples of Christ which began work in 1883 had only four missionaries throughout most of this period, though there were eight after 1888. One church at Akita with an ordained pastor and one helper constituted the national force. This meant that the slow growth of the Disciples was due to an inadequate mission machine because of its late arrival and the poverty of its missionary and national forces. Besides, the missionaries at Akita were reported to have recognized that "they were somewhat on the fringe of things so far as influence in the Japanese Empire was concerned."[77] They missed out on the Western vogue of the 1880's by being located in the rural district. Tokyo was the intellectual and cultural center and Akita was too far removed from the capital and any other major center of westernization.

The growth among most churches during the second half of the 1880's was more distinct than the first. This was especially true among the fastest growing churches and we must ask why. From Table 1 through 3, it is evident that the churches generally improved their mission machines during the second half. There were more missionary reinforcements. More national leaders were trained. And all denominations except the bottom two almost doubled the number of their organized churches by the end of this period. In addition to the improved mission machines, there was another more direct cause for the post-1885 rapid growth. With the popular demand for representative government, the oligarchs secured the emperor's consent to issue an Imperial Rescript "pledging that constitutional government would be 'given' by the Emperor to the people of Japan by the year 1889."[78] Hirobumi Ito, then head of the Home Ministry, was assigned to make a study in preparation for the new constitution. He went to Europe and was most impressed by the situation he found in Bismarckian Germany. He returned home in 1885 and was appointed the Premier of Japan. It was he who became convinced that

> if any progress was to be made in the direction of revising the Unequal Trade Treaties, the west not only had to be convinced that Japan possessed modern forms of government, but that she at least took a permissive attitude toward Christianity.[79]

Thus, Christianity for the next few years received the sanction of the officialdom. The two largest denominations, more particularly the Congregational Church, were blessed by the addition of many men and women of high social status into their memberships. This blessing would later prove to be a point of much concern for the church as we shall see in the following chapter.

3. Summary: the structure of growth. In our concluding remark, we shall make a few observations concerning the structure of growth which prevailed during this period.

First, we can safely conclude from the above discussion that the sector of society which was most open to the West was at the same time most responsive to the Christian faith. During the period of the 1880's, the upper and middle class intellectuals in urban districts showed remarkable affinity to Western ideology. By 1889, thirty percent of the church membership came from the old *samurai* class and the rest from the upper middle classes made up of rich farmers and merchants, school teachers, technicians, and office workers.[80] Particularly, the two largest churches had notable response from the upper class, though this would remain in the annals of Japanese church history as the only period in which Protestantism had any significant response from that class.

Thomas, Sugii, and other sources all agree that the largest number of converts were students, predominantly those from the mission schools. Should the number of post-graduate converts be counted, the major way into the church in Japan could be characterized by the school approach during this period.

Second, the fastest growing churches during this period were better equipped to take advantage of Japan's unusual openness to the West. The field was ripened by the revolution of the seventies, by the progress on the agrarian-industrial spectrum, by relative freedom from fear of foreign domination, and more specifically by the pressure for treaty revision. These churches were in a position to capitalize on this ripeness of the field and Japan's readiness to absorb Western influences by their improved mission machines and special emphasis. Congregational and Presbyterian Churches had the greatest number of missionaries; trained the national forces quickly; organized more churches with many of them already self-supporting; concentrated their churchly forces in strategic places; emphasized education, self-support, and simplicity of worship; and attracted many able nationals within their memberships with their representative form of government. Other churches with similar qualities were able to grow faster than those less endowed by them.

Third, brief mention must be made regarding the relationship of revival to church growth. Earlier we stated that a series of revivals followed the missionary and national Christian conventions of 1883 and that many Christians were revived and through them others came to accept the faith. Uncritical reading of historical documents about the revivals of the 1880's might incline the reader to reach an erroneous conclusion that the great growth of the 1880's was singularly caused by the revivals. One gets such an impression by going over the narratives and accounts of some individual cases. More careful reading of the documents, however, helps us correct this error. The facts are as follows. The "fires of spiritual 'revival'" began to burn among the foreign community in Yokohama in 1883.[81] They spread first to some of the girls' schools in the city and then to the Methodist-related Aoyama Gakuin in Tokyo. The flames of spiritual fires spilled over other places such as Kyoto, Sendai, Nagoya, Nagasaki, and Oita in Kyushu.[82] In each place, a small group of young Christians became spiritually vivified and those influenced by them professed their faith. "One of the most marked of these," wrote Cary, "was in the Doshisha."[83] It is reported[84] that several Christian students met in a daily meeting about the first of March, 1884. By March 16, the whole school, as the story goes, was influenced by this spiritual surge. But school authorities, especially the missionaries, tried to prevent the students from becoming extravagant in their behavior by urging

> as strongly as they knew how, that the regularity of school life be maintained as regards studies, meals, exercise, and sleep; that the prayer-meetings be held early in the evening and be rigidly restricted to one hour; and that special pains be taken to secure quiet during the evening.[85]

So the result was that, after some two hundred students were baptized,[86] things returned to normal.

In other words, the revivals of the 1880's took place mostly in schools at different times, each lasting for a short duration, and did not develop into a spiritual combustion sweeping the entire nation in one big blaze. "Revival" meant in those days a gracious blessing of God's spirit, sweeping churches and schools and leading many in both communities to deeper dedication and also to new and more open commitment to Christ. Revival did trigger some conversions, among sodalities of students, but was confined to the schools. It was, therefore, unable to spread to families, for students residing in dormitories were not in living contact with their families. The one-by-one pattern also kept most revivals from lighting fires of faith in extended families and village clans.

Japan's openness to the West definitely favored church growth among the denominations which were more equipped to ride the wave of Western popularity. But there came a time when things Western fell into disrepute, and the churches were variously affected by this sudden transition in the mood of the nation. The effects of this hard line period upon the churches will be discussed in the next chapter.

CHAPTER III

The Hard Line, 1890-1902

Socio-Cultural Setting

The period between 1890 and 1902 is often reported as difficult for church growth in Japan. An anti-Western and essentially anti-Christian climate prevailed in the decade following 1889. The spirit of openness which facilitated popular response to Christianity during the 1880's was hardened by various causes. Yet not all the churches were affected equally by these environmental factors which were factors external to the church. Some churches were able to advance in spite of numerous socio-cultural obstacles, while others revealed distinct reduction in the rate of growth. The general problem posed in this chapter can be phrased as follows: "To what extent and under what circumstances do environmental factors effect church growth?" This is the problem which needs to be probed throughout this book, but the period under review presents the model case *par excellence*.

The first section of this chapter describes the environmental factors which are commonly acknowledged as having caused the reaction against Christianity. The second section presents two salient facts related to the growth of the churches. The third section delves into the causes of these phenomena so that we may delimit the effects of environmental factors upon church growth.

1. Failure of treaty revision as the catalyst. For various reasons discussed in the previous chapter, Japan was extremely open to the West during the 1880's. The government took initiative in reforming every aspect of its life to achieve the goal of making Japan rich and strong. One big obstacle lay in the way of progress. The "one thing needful," as the Japanese understood it, was the revision of unequal treaties. To rectify this obstacle, Japan launched a massive campaign to impress upon Western neighbors that it was a modern state and was entitled to be an equal member of the family of nations. Western ways including religion became popular among certain sectors of society. Just as the pressure for treaty revision inculcated the adoption of Western manners, customs, and ideology by the Japanese, "the event which precipitated the reaction against Western civilization and thereby the Protestant regression was the failure of the treaty negotiations."[1]

Following a series of unsuccessful negotiations, a new attempt was made with the coming of Shigenobu Okuma to the position of Foreign Minister. The provision regarding collegiate courts was responsible for the failure of an earlier negotiation in 1887. What was offensive to the nationalistic-minded Japanese was that Western judges had to be included in dealing with the cases involving foreign subjects, a provision which implied the undermining of Japan's judicial autonomy. Okuma's revised plan for collegiate courts did not satisfy his political opponents. On October 18, 1889, one Tsuneki Kurushima attempted to take Okuma's life with a bomb. Okuma was badly hurt. The assailant committed suicide, and the assailed was forced to resign when the Cabinet dissolved.[2] Thus the failure of treaty revision in 1889 played the role of a catalyst which set off various indigenous reactions against the alien religion. In addition, some factors of foreign origin lent their force to distract the mind of Japan from Christianity. These environmental factors will be discussed below.

2. Factors which created the anti-Christian climate. The main source for the following discussion is Copeland's doctoral dissertation, "The Crisis of Protestant Missions to Japan, 1889-1900," Chapter II. The author in turn depended largely, but not exclusively, upon Thomas, "A History of Protestant Christianity in Japan, 1883-1889," Chapter IV. The purpose of this section is to describe

the commonly acknowledged causes for the reaction against Christianity during the 1890's. Therefore, we shall make use of Copeland's extended analysis of the decade of crisis for Japanese Protestantism. The first six factors are essentially his, and we shall add two others.

First, the anti-Christian climate was created by "the rising tide of Japanese nationalism."[3] The conservative segments of the Japanese society never fully shared the pro-Western fervor of the 1880's. There was some active opposition, notably from the Buddhists, even at the height of Japan's infatuation with the West. In the main, these conservative elements were hushed and submerged in the interest of obtaining the most desired goal of treaty revision. But the failure of negotiations in 1889 brought the conservative reaction to the surface. The protest against denationalization became the burning torch which guided the path of conservatism. The organization in 1885 of the True Teachings Club *(Seikyo Sha)* was the beginning of the "Japanese National Essence" movement,[4] and after the event of 1889 the influence of the movement became magnified even in such fields as art and history. It was a movement away from Western ideas and customs and a movement back to Japanese ideologies. Christianity, which was so closely identified with the blessings of westernization during the previous decade, was now made "a scapegoat in the resentment against the West."[5]

Second, the anti-Christian climate was created by the revival of Japanese religions.[6] During the period of Western popularity, the influence of the dominant religions of Japan appeared to be lessened. As Thomas stated,

> Confucianism lacked vitality, Buddhism was moribund, and Shinto, except for its concern with court rituals, was primarily occupied with the routine observance of traditional festivals, esoteric rites and the sales of charms.[7]

But these religions soon "proved much more virile and firmly rooted than the missionaries suspected."[8] With the rising tide of nationalism, the three religions which helped strengthen traditional values and loyalties regained their prominence. Confucian ideals of loyalty and filial piety were incorporated in the Imperial Rescript on Education issued in 1890. The oligarchy aimed at the ideological unity of Japan through the emperor institution based on Shinto. The Shintoists who "found imperial sanction for their religion in the Rescript on Education"[9] renewed their religious activity. Earlier, we have noted that Buddhism among the religions of Japan was most hostile to Christianity during the period of Western popularity. Now the Buddhists chose the posture of aggressive offense rather than that of defense.[10] Under the slogan, "Revere the Emperor, worship Buddha, and unite on the main points of the Buddhist faith," they challenged anyone who demonstrated disloyalty to the emperor and opposition to Buddhism regardless of his position in society.[11] To the proponents of these religions, Christianity was a foreign religion antagonistic to the spirit of Japan, and Christians appeared to be unpatriotic. The universalism of Christ religion became suspect in the interest of the particularism of emperor worship; Christ was considered to be the emperor's rival.

Third, the anti-Christian climate was created by the political agitation of the 1890's.[12] The early years of the decade of the 1890's were the period of political innovation and turbulence in Japan. The much awaited Constitution was promulgated in 1889. The Diet first met in 1890. Heretofore, the Japanese had been unaccustomed to the system of electing public officials, and the subject of election was the talk of the day. The tug of war between the Cabinet and Diet brought about frequent changes of personnel in political leadership and served to excite the general populace. The Sino-Japanese War of 1894-1895 poured oil on the existing fire of national excitement. The people's preoccupation with the concerns of political life diverted their attention from Christianity and created the climate unfavorable to its growth.

Fourth, the anti-Christian climate was created by the financial condition of Japan.[13] The economic crisis of the early 1890's was caused by the adverse effects of industrial and commercial revolution, by the disasters such as earthquakes and floods, and by the war with China, which necessitated a sharp rise in taxation.[14] This crisis "helped to bring about decreased enrollments in Christian schools, lowered attendance at church services and reduced contributions for Christian work."[15] The Protestant movement in Japan drew a large number of converts from the mission schools, and their decreased enrollments definitely narrowed the avenue of ingathering. The low rate of attendance at church services lessened not only the zeal and activity of the existing members but also the number of contacts with prospective Christians. Furthermore, reduction in the amount of financial contributions had a staggering ill effect upon the growth of self-supporting churches.

In addition, materialism caused by the economic prosperity which followed the war with China distracted the attention of the people from spiritual matters.

> Some Christians were so busy that they neglected religious duties; those engaged in manufactures found it easy to invent excuses for not observing the Sabbath; and others yielded to the temptations that beset those that are in haste to become rich.[16]

Even the ministers were not aloof from these commercial and materialistic influences. Many of them traded their education (which had a high commercial value) for a more remunerative employment. Also "commercialism, theological doubts, and a general loss of earnestness combined to reduce greatly the number of young men studying in the theological schools."[17]

Fifth, the anti-Christian climate was created by "a series of events which discredited the professedly Christian nations in the eyes of Japan."[18] The Japanese have often judged Christianity by the behavior of Western nations because of their inability to isolate religion from politics. The unwillingness of the West to grant judicial and tariff autonomy infuriated the people of Japan. Japanese resentment against Western nations and Christianity was prompted by evidences of Western imperialism: the annexation of Port Hamilton by England and of Hawaii and the Phillippines by America, the seizure of Indo-China by France and of Kiaochow by Germany.[19] Unchristian conduct of some Westerners in Japan and abroad further discredited their religion. There were many incidents of an undesirable nature involving foreigners in treaty ports. Japanese traveling abroad reported that Western nations were not morally superior, as some missionaries claimed them to be.[20]

Sixth, the anti-Christian climate was created by the infiltration of anti-Christian thought from the West.[21] The introduction of the works of such philosophers as Spencer, Mill, and Tyndall and of Darwinism helped turn the Japanese away from the religion of supernaturalism preached by the missionaries.[22] Scientism captured the interest of educated Japanese. Critics of Christianity such as Paine and Ingersoll also exerted influence upon like-minded Japanese and damaged the missionary cause.

Seventh, the anti-Christian climate was created by the strict enforcement of the terms of the treaties.[23] Advocates of "strict enforcement" in the Diet thought that Western powers might make concessions to the treaty revision if their hands were forced. They suggested that foreigners be subjected to the letter within the terms of the treaties. Such a suggestion was a cause for embarrassment to the central government, and the Diet dissolved. By 1894, the plea for a stronger foreign policy not only won a large portion of the Diet but also swept the country. It may very well be conjectured that the decision to engage in a war with China was made "in order to silence the political-party opposition."[24]

At any rate, the government's hard line policy — be it local or central — made missionary travels, residency in the interior, and property-holding more difficult. Restrictions upon missionary travels and residency in the interior had a more potent ill effect upon the spread of the faith. Until then, government officials had been very lenient in granting passports and permits for these purposes. Permission to travel and reside in the interior had been easily obtainable provided that the missionary was engaged in scientific research, seeking the recovery of his health, or employed by a school or an individual for the purpose of teaching English.[25] The missionaries utilized such opportunities to preach the gospel. Now, though temporarily, officials, especially those in prefectural governments, girded up their loins and hardened their attitudes towards the missionaries. Getting passports and permits became more difficult. The growth of Protestantism suffered to the extent that the missionaries were pinned down in port cities and foreign settlements and were not allowed to travel or reside in the interior.

Eighth, the anti-Christian climate was created by the resystematization of the family ethic.[26] We have already mentioned in another context that there was a real confusion of values in the transition period from feudal to modern society. Certain segments within the Japanese society were heavily influenced by Western ideology, and many persons under the duress of this confusion turned to Christianity in search of an internal authority. The sovereignty of the Meiji government itself was unstable because of this confusion of values at that time. "Therefore," says Sumiya, "in the 1880's the government concentrated its efforts on the formation of a culturally and politically unified society with the emperor in the center."[27] The Constitution of 1889 and more particularly the Rescript on Education of 1890 validated the claim that the emperor as head of the national community embodied the will of the people and was thus the basis of all ethical conduct.[28] The genius of the Meiji government made the family ideology the foundation for the emperor system. "The family and the nation were considered as concentric communities, with the nation being an extension of the family."[29] The emperor was the father, and all his subjects were his faithful children. The family system, the cornerstone of traditionalism in Japan, regained its strength after 1889 under the new emperor institution, if it was weakened at all during the 1880's. And as the family ethic was resystematized along the line of loyalty to the emperor, liberal Western ideology and Christianity were forced to retreat.

These eight environmental factors helped create the anti-Christian atmosphere of the 1890's. Later, we shall examine to what extent and under what circumstances these factors can be claimed as having had direct influence upon church growth.

Ecclesiastical Setting

After introducing the arrival of the rest of our eight churches, we shall establish two salient facts regarding the growth of the churches: (1) some churches overcame and others succumbed to the anti-Christian climate; (2) reduction in the rate of growth among some churches was caused primarily not by lack of converts but by the severity of membership loss.

1. Two against the storm. Southern Baptist and Adventist Churches braved their way into Japan against the storm of anti-Westernism.

The would-be pioneer missionaries of the Southern Baptists, Rev. and Mrs. J.Q.A. Rohrer, set sail for Japan on the *Edwin Forest* in 1860. The ill-fated vessel was lost at sea and the missionaries never reached their destination.[30] The Civil War and reconstruction delayed the Southern Baptist representation in Japan until November 5, 1889 when J.W. McCollum and J.A. Brunson, accompanied by their wives, arrived at Yokohama.[31] Though begun in late 1889, the year 1890 is generally accepted as the beginning of the mission in Japan; it was the year when the mission was first organized.[32] The first station was opened in Osaka in 1891 with fifteen members. This was later transferred to the American Baptists when a comity agreement was reached between them relegating the island of Kyushu to the newcomer.[33]

The mission emphasized the policy of direct evangelism. Though a day school was conducted in 1893, it was soon discontinued. Failure to maintain educational work, according to one author, was directly responsible for the lack of able leaders among Southern Baptists. He wrote:

> As we look back and watch the development of our Japan Mission, we realize our mistake in failing to continue educational work in those early days. The missionaries, through the years, gave private instruction to those who desired to preach the gospel, but depended on the Government and heathen schools to train our church leaders.[34]

At the end of the 1890's, the mission reported:

> There were eight missionaries, six evangelists, one ordained pastor, 75 members (scattered over a 50-mile radius) in one organized church at Moji, and 11 preaching stations in major cities.[35]

And the communicant membership in 1902 numbered one hundred and twenty. The Southern Baptist mission during this period worked in a more conservative region with the handicap of lean missionary and national forces. Lack of funds and a sole emphasis on direct evangelism deprived the mission of its growth through educational means.

The last of the eight to arrive in Japan was the Seventh-Day Adventist Church. The Adventist mission to the Japanese had its introduction among the Japanese immigrants in San Francisco in the early nineties. A mission school was started there, and a number of its students were converted. Some of them further advanced their education by going to Healdsburg College.[36] When the College was closed in 1896, its former president and student, W.C. Grainger and T.H. Okohira respectively, sailed for Japan to commence missionary work there. November 16, 1896 marked the beginning of the Adventist mission on Japanese soil. After careful study of the situation, the missionaries decided to work along educational lines. They conducted the Shiba Bible School in Tokyo which soon reached the attendance of sixty. Most of these were students attending regular schools in the city who wished to acquire the knowledge of English. Within a year, the first church, with a membership of thirteen, was organized in the same city.[37] By the close of this period, the communicant membership reached fifty-five.

During the early years, the work suffered much from the frequent change in missionary personnel. The missionary and ordained national forces gradually built up in the course of time, but the Adventist Church did not have a large staff throughout its history. The 1936 figure of thirty-five was the maximum for the missionary force and the 1937 figure of nineteen for the ordained nationals. The church also enjoyed steady but never spectacular growth. After 1905, a series of tent meetings were held in Tokyo and in other cities. Each summer a team of workers visited "a city of some size which had in the previous winter been worked by canvassers."[38] But "the immediate results of these tent efforts have never been large."[39] A good result depended upon a systematic follow-up of those who showed interest in the public meeting. Of the Adventist respondents, it was reported in 1925 that "the younger generation [was] the freest to accept the gospel" and, further, that:

> The principles of the feudal system, by which the rights of the individual were subordinated to the interests of the family, the village, and the nation, still prevail generally in Japan, especially in the rural districts.[40]

In the Adventist mission as in others, the persons who readily responded to the faith were those young people who were detached from the traditional mores of the society.

Besides educational and evangelistic work, the mission operated a sanitarium at Kobe which was a great service to the missionary contingents of all denominations. Later a similar work was begun for the Japanese.

All through the years, more than half of the church members came from the Tokyo area and another large portion from the Osaka-Kobe district. Thus young urbanites predominated in the membership of this mission. It appears that the mission with a relatively small staff diversified its efforts too thinly to yield a large response.

2. Facts of growth differentials and membership leakage. Figure 1 (p. 6) partly confirms and partly denies the report that the period between 1890 and 1902 was difficult for church growth in Japan. It was a "difficult period" for Congregational and Presbyterian Churches, but others found it rather favorable. The Methodists gained slight but significant growth. Episcopal and American Baptist Churches more than doubled their memberships. Bishop Henry Tucker calls this an "era of notable progress" for the Episcopal Church.[41] Some smaller groups had much greater proportionate increases. The Disciples of Christ more than tripled its membership, and even those missions which entered the field during the 1890's registered distinct percentage growth, though small in absolute quantity. Perhaps, Copeland was right when he wrote, "The reaction appeared to be more critical than it was because it was con-

trasted with the remarkable growth of the 1880's."[42] The truth of this statement may be attested by the fact that

> those missions which entered at the time of the reaction and those which had experienced relatively slow growth in the decade which preceded did not express so much discouragement during the reaction as did the groups which had previously recorded such large numbers of conversions.[43]

The two largest denominations, especially the Congregational Church, experienced a distinct setback.

Why did two churches stand still and others continue to grow? Many answers are possible, which we sum up by saying that, while the climate caused by the 1889 reaction to Westernism and essentially against Christianity was certainly unfavorable, several churches overcame their climate but two succumbed to it. In the following section, we shall examine the reasons why the two largest churches experienced sharp reduction in their rate of growth.

A huge backdoor or membership leakage naturally has an unavoidable ill effect upon the growth of the church. Concerning the slow growth of Protestantism during the 1890's, a missionary historian stated that "this was not so much from lack of baptisms as from heavy losses through removals, withdrawals, and discipline."[44] In fact, the Presbyterian Church, whose missionary he was, took in about 6,600 persons during the ten years from 1890 to 1899 only to net about 600. Thus, "out of 6,600, 6,000 had disappeared!"[45] This statement by Pieters must not be misunderstood. To be more accurate, it should read as follows: the Presbyterian Church during the ten-year period lost six thousand members, and this number was ninety percent of six and a half thousand, the number baptized during the same period. But certainly, many of those who disappeared may have been earlier members and the leakage was not primarily of new members. It is within reason to conclude that the Presbyterian Church underwent massive membership leakage during 1890-1899.

From available facts related to our churches, we shall test the missionary historian's important insight that the Protestant movement suffered "not so much from lack of baptisms as from heavy losses."

The following table shows the number of adult baptisms (or confirmations) among six of our eight churches. Due to their recent arrival, Southern Baptist and Adventist Churches are excluded from the survey.

Table 4
Adult Baptisms, 1888-1900

Church	1888	1891	1894	1897	1900
Episcopal	889	466	508	421	722
Presbyterian	1,937	844	603	730	700
A. Baptist	207	251	236	183	176
Congregational	2,801	1,040	670	420	519
Methodist	1,298	669	549	634	629
Disciples	50	42	55	50	138

Source: Compiled from *Tokyo Conference Report,* pp. 990, 991.

The number of baptisms in 1891 and in each of the following years was roughly half of the 1888 figure in Episcopal, Presbyterian, Congregational, and Methodist Churches. In comparison with the receptivity of the latter half of the 1880's, the effect of the hard line period was more markedly felt among these large churches. But even then, the gains which had been achieved during the "difficult period" were actually quite substantial and cannot be said that the churches lacked baptisms. One of the determining factors related to the structure òf slow growth was severe membership leakage. All churches in Japan suffered from it, some more severely than others. Table 5 graphically reveals this fact.

Table 5
Annual Average Rate of Membership Leakage 1890-1902

Church	Average annual gain: adult baptisms$_a$	Average annual gain: Communicants$_b$	Percentage of leakage (%)$_c$
Episcopal	529	282	47
Presbyterian	719	115	84
A. Baptist	211	84	61
Congregational	662	42	94
Methodist	620	143	77
Disciples	71	37	48

a. From Table 4 (p. 74) an average annual gain in adult baptisms from 1891 to 1900 has been computed for each of our six churches.

b. An average annual gain in the communicant membership of each church can be obtained since Appendixes A through F list absolute figures for 1890 and 1902. Where these figures are lacking, we have utilized the carefully measured original graph comprising Figure 1 (p. 6). Thus, reasonable approximations are made for Episcopal (5,700 in 1902); for Presbyterian (9,000 in 1890 and 10,500 in 1902); and for Disciples (200 in 1890).

c. If the Episcopal Church netted 282 out of 529 in any given year, this simply means that the church conserved 53% and lost 47% of the number baptized that year. Of course, many of those lost may have been Christians for several years. The annual average rates of membership leakage of other churches have been calculated in the same way. We have every reason to believe that the rates of membership leakage of other churches during this period were somewhat similar to those given in this column.

What an astounding fact this is! The Congregational Church lost 620 members, and this number was ninety-four percent of 662, the number baptized in a given year. Some of those lost may have been from the persons added to the church that year, but many from those who were Christians for several years. No church with losses of this magnitude can grow. Even the Episcopal Church, which retained most, lost in essence forty-seven members for every one hundred, the number equal to those baptized that year. All churches in Japan obviously suffered much from membership leakage, but the largest two which grew fastest during the previous decade declined most in their rate of growth during this period. Should the churches be able to conserve their existing memberships, certainly with the annual additions through baptisms, Congregational and Presbyterian Churches would have retained growth similar to that of the previous decade, and other churches would have seen a sharper rise in their lines of growth. The major problem was primarily severe membership leakage and not lack of baptisms.

Church Growth Interpretation

Two salient facts projected in the previous section must now receive rigorous analysis, the purpose of which is to give limits to the effects of environmental factors upon church growth.

1. Analysis of growth differentials. There were two major trends of growth during this period: (1) the Congregational and Presbyterian plateaus and (2) the continued growth of other churches. By examining why particularly the two largest churches underwent reduction in their rate of growth, we hope to make clear why others were less affected by the ills vexing the afflicted.

First, we reiterate the point already made. Congregational and Presbyterian Churches had the highest rate of membership leakage. Second, Congregational and Presbyterian mission schools experienced marked decrease in enrollments, but the schools operated by other churches apparently did not.[46]

The crisis in mission schools was caused by various factors. The adverse economic condition of the early 1890's, as mentioned earlier, made some families unable to keep their children in school. Also, after the promulgation of the Imperial Rescript on Education, many Christian students found subtle and blunt persecution unbearable. After 1892, the loyalty of Christians to the emperor was

openly challenged by a prominent anti-Christian exponent. Tetsuj-
iro Inoue, professor at the Tokyo Imperial University, wrote:

> Our Imperial Rescript on Education is based entirely upon nationalism
> (kokka shugi), but the Christians in our country have not received this
> [rescript] well. We have had cases in the schools of [Christian]
> students refusing to respect the Imperial picture. The logical conclu-
> sion of this is that Christianity is absolutely anti-national . . . Since it
> places emphasis upon the equality of all before God, it does not accept
> reverence for the Emperor and consequently places no value upon the
> idea of loyalty. It cares not the least whether the state deteriorates.[47]

Furthermore, the government improved its schools during this decade when it recognized that, in order to complete the scheme of
modernization, it had

> to strengthen the public education system and to outnumber private
> schools, including Christian institutions, where that Western
> liberalism which the government did not want spread further in Japan
> was still a powerful spirit.[48]

The reason why two churches particularly suffered decreased
enrollments in their schools may be that since many of their students
were more able and nationalistic-minded, they either quit or transferred to government schools.

Third, Congregational and Presbyterian Churches had a large
share of "fair-weather Christians"[49] in government circles and
among the upper class. Many of them joined the church during the
second half of the 1880's, when the tide of pro-Westernism favored
Christianity and especially when they thought that the acceptance
of Christianity would help induce the Western powers to grant Japan
the desired treaty revision. But as soon as the tide shifted or with the
breakdown of the negotiations, they were easily swallowed up by
high waves of national hostility and anti-Christian sentiments.
"Many of the upper class who had taken interest in the faith fell
away since it was no longer the thing to do."[50]

Fourth, the evangelistic zeal and efforts of Congregational and
Presbyterian Churches were tragically curtailed by the following
two factors. First, the "clamor for independence" in national affairs
was echoed in matters ecclesiastical. The critical problem arose in
the area of mission-church relationships. The desire for judicial and
tariff autonomy in national affairs was converted into the desire for
ecclesiastical autonomy. Tension between missionaries and national leaders was unavoidable. Speer reported in 1897:

> Some of the small, strictly disciplined bodies would probably say that
> while the general temper has been seriously felt, they had not met any
> grave defection.[51]

But, what was "ironical" was that the churches with "the lightest
measure of missionary control" least likely to incur the anger of
nationalism should suffer most from this movement for
independence.[52] Once again, Congregational and Presbyterian
Churches proved to be most vulnerable.[53] Thus, the internal dissen-
sions caused the churches to turn inwardly to their own problems
and to shy away from their outward responsibility of spreading the
faith.

Second, skepticism and radical views from the West took the fire
out of the evangelistic enterprises. The fact that Congregational and
Presbyterian Churches had, within their constituencies, persons
who were "better educated than the others and in closer touch with
intellectual and theological currents"[54] explains why they were
more readily affected by the infiltration of anti-Christian thought
and radical theology. The so-called "New Theology" penetrated
most among the Congregationalists, particularly of Doshisha.[55] Dr.
Davis, a Congregational missionary, wrote an article in 1897 which
reveals the spiritual condition of the Japanese church though mostly
speaking from the knowledge of his own church.

> Men whom God has used in former years to build up large churches
> have some of them made shipwreck of their faith, and others are
> denying the supernatural and doubting the personality of
> God . . . The old Gospel, the Gospel that Christ preached, and that
> Paul preached, is the only Gospel that can save the millions of the
> nations who know not God. Another Gospel has been preached here.
> Some of the Japanese leaders have told the churches that the founda-
> tions of Christianity which the missionaries have laid must all be swept
> away and new foundations laid: the Bible and Christ have been
> disparaged; the atonement denied and a humanitarian gospel
> preached while the infant church has been stunned and bewildered
> for five years not knowing what to believe.[56]

Speer judges that "no other orthodox Church has suffered nearly so
severely as the Kumiai [Congregational Church]" and that the Presbyterian Church, closest of all churches to the Kumiai, has been
most affected by the same general influence.[57] During the 1880's,
missionaries and Japanese Christians were driven by deep theological convictions. They were actively engaged in evangelism with the
burning passion and rock-ribbed faith in the sufficiency of Christ
and the unsearchable riches which are in Him. The cold theology of

the 1890's and the influence of skepticism chilled the passion of the church and immobilized its evangelistic efforts.

The decreased evangelistic fervor and efforts gave birth to a monolithic leadership structure which contributed to the structure of slow growth. Of its birth, Cary wrote:

> Whereas all of the Christians had once felt the responsibility for telling others about their new faith, and had been earnest in leading their friends to accept it, they were not inclined to leave the work of propagation almost entirely to the pastors and evangelists.[58]

This pattern of church leadership becomes firmly regimented in the twentieth century, and we will have occasion to refer to it in another context.

2. Analysis of membership leakage. The huge backdoor plagued all churches alike, though the two largest suffered more pronounced damage. What produced this unwholesome phenomenon of membership loss? The partial answer has already been given. We maintain that what we called environmental factors were more the causes of membership leakage than those directly affecting the decrease in the number of converts. They were the causes external to the church. While reserving our conceptualization for a later discourse, we shall introduce further causes rising out of the conditions internal to the church.

First, the character of the majority of the Protestant constituency was most vulnerable to the influence of physical migration.

> It is an undisputable fact that the great majority of Christians come from that class of people whose duties, public or private, take them from under the influence of the ancestral home and its surroundings: in other words, the migrating population.[59]

The salaried men are subjected to frequent moves from one place to another during their careers. The auxiliaries to the salaried class are students. Many became Christian while attending school. An outstanding fact was that a large proportion of students in the mission schools accepted the faith by the time of their graduation. While a fair percentage of them remained in the same city where the school was located, the rest moved away to another city or town to seek employment. Frequent moves, demanded of their careers, furnished an easy alibi to let churchly affairs slide, and the less committed found refuge in the anonymity of the new environment. Some denominations were widely dispersed throughout the country, but at this time, the number of churches in each denomination was too few to be effective as a buffer against leakage resulting from membership mobility.

Second, the character of the majority of Protestant constituency was most susceptible to the intellectual current of the day which largely contributed to the intellectual migration out of the church. The early converts to Christianity were those within the Japanese society who were least bound to the traditional mores and loyalties of the ancestral homes. They were relatively free to accept and reject the things of the West and were very sensitive to the changing tides of Western thought. They often moved from one fad or ideology to another with ease unimaginable to those enslaved by the traditional modes of regimentation. This is not difficult to understand. A great number of Japanese Christians came into the church as either student converts or post-graduate converts. In either case, they cultivated an attitude of mind that Christianity was something to be studied like any other subject. When they graduated from the mission school or after going to church for a few years, they also 'graduated' from Christianity. Just as easily as they caught hold of a new faith (often without definite personal experience of its transforming power), they were quick to let it go when the current fad went out of style or the new one competed for their allegiance.

Third, the unique mosaic of membership in the average local congregation in Japan helped widen the backdoor. An average local church contained within its membership a large number of singles and half families (where only a husband or wife was a Christian). This type of membership structure within the church fostered membership leakage. How this was so is partly explained by McGavran as follows:

> In India many have been baptized *with their families and kinsmen.* They stay "Christians" even if their fervency dies down; whereas in Japan most converts come in without their families and kinfolk, so that when ardor flags they are pulled back into the non-Christian orbit.[60]

Furthermore, even without the reduction of fervency the Christians generally found it difficult to keep their faith alive against the traditional family system. Becoming a Christian often meant a declaration of war against family and ancestral heritage. The young convert received practically no encouragement at home, if not active opposition. Unless the head of the family himself became a Christian, the sons and daughters were not allowed to love Christ more than their ancestral deities. The sense of alienation which the convert experienced by cutting "deep and dear emotional ties with his traditional milieu"[61] frequently drove him to a breaking point where the weight of family tradition crushed the growth of an alien faith. The church was a colony of individuals uprooted from their homes because of their faith. For many, it virtually became the only source of comfort and warmth which the natural families were no longer willing to give to their delinquent members. Rather than providing a home for these spiritual refugees, the church had a tendency to overemphasize the one-sided, vertical relationship and confrontation between the believer and his God. The church sometimes lacked genuine fellowship among its members and its activities were narrowly confined to Sunday worship.

Young Christian women faced an added problem of marriage to non-Christians. Marriages were mostly "arranged" before World War II and rarely could a Christian marry another. Many Christian women chose to remain single rather than to marry and jeopardize their faith. Once married, young Christian men had a better chance of guiding their non-Christian wives to the faith than young Christian women their husbands.

Fourth, out of intense loyalty to his home church, the convert, upon moving to another city, was inclined to shy away from joining another church. One missionary wrote at the turn of the century as follows:

> Influenced by a not un-natural sentimentality, many are loth to remove their membership from the place of their spiritual birth; and under the present non-cooperative arrangement, the pastor or missionary hesitates to urge them to leave their own churches and seek membership in another denomination. For a time they are kept in touch with the pastor or missionary by letter, but sooner or later communication ceases; and their whereabouts becoming unknown, the record is marked "dropped".[62]

The missionary argued that the many denominations caused migrants to remain loyal to their own and to refuse to affiliate with a nearby church of another denomination. Therefore, if denominationalism were to be abolished by forming a United Church, the problem of denominationalism and consequently that of membership leakage would be eliminated or at least lessened. While this was no doubt a reason, it could easily be overestimated. The United Church of Christ in Japan experiences today much loss by migration. The more important cause appears to have been intense loyalty to "the place of their spiritual birth." Even where there was a church of his own denomination, his intense loyalty to the place of his spiritual birth prevented him from joining the church and being active in it. After moving to the new city, he would keep in touch with his home pastor for a while, but the various pressures causing membership leakage would soon catch up with him, and he would become a loss to the church.

Fifth, insufficient pastoral care left the flock spiritually starving.[63] There were many reasons for this. The church usually demonstrated its active interest in the persons until they professed their faith, but often neglected the post-baptismal care of the flock. While the educated parish required a highly trained ministry, the average Japanese minister was too much of a theologian and not enough of a pastor. Though the parishioner was able to hear a highly intellectual discourse from the pulpit, he was largely left to himself as to the application of theology in the day to day encounter in the often hostile, non-Christian society. The wide spread of members in the city also made calling time consuming. According to Cary, the rapid growth of the church during the previous decade exhausted the church's energy[64] and consequently the parishioners received little or no pastoral care. In addition, there was around this time a distinct shift from the more dynamic ministry involving active lay participation to the more linear structure of church leadership with sole dependence upon the paid ministry. The church failed to make creative use of responsible laity in the area of pastoral care. Thus, insufficient pastoral care for whatever reason worked against conserving the existing membership.

Sixth, some Christians simply grew cold in their faith and left the church. The radical shift in theology towards liberalism during the 1890's caused much theological upheaval in the Protestant constituency, and many Christians abandoned their faith altogether. Many new converts were disappointed in the church because Christians were not what they thought them to be. Some left the church because they felt that Christianity did not meet their needs.

But there are other reasons. Perhaps, the church failed to instruct and train its members in matters spiritual and some members were simply unable to maintain their spiritual glow. Or, the church's high moral standards forced some Christians to stay out of the church, and eventually they were lost to the world. Morioka's study reveals some of the church's practices during the 1890's. He writes:

> The Christian moral reform movement . . . concentrated on the
> prohibition of smoking and drinking and the strict observance of
> monogamy. Any one who did not terminate relations with his con-
> cubines after conversion, or who divorced his wife without proper
> grounds, or who associated with prostitutes, or acted in any other way
> contrary to the dictates of Christian sexual morality was excluded from
> the Church and deprived of the privilege of taking holy communion.[65]

Anyone who fell into what the church considered to be sin — be it
smoking, drinking, man or woman trouble, or whatever— withdrew
from the church fellowship until such time as he reconciled with his
personal problem, but often he found it difficult to return to the fold
and remained outside it.

Our church growth interpretation took us through the analyses of
growth differentials and membership leakage. The remainder of this
chapter will devote itself to the conceptualization of the relationship
between environmental factors and church growth.

3. Effects of environmental factors upon church growth. The
period of the 1890's witnessed a reaction to the unleashed pro-
Westernism af the 1880's and along with it the hardening of the
spirit of tolerance towards Christianity. The two largest churches
found this period difficult for church growth, while others apparently did not. In fact, they demonstrated continuous growth with
varying degrees. We have attempted our version of what really
caused the growth differentials among these churches especially by
contrasting the Congregational-Presbyterian plateaus from the lines
of continued growth. When the environmental factors commonly
known as having spurred anti-Christian sentiments are examined
against those which produced the growth differentials, some important insights emerge which will delineate the influence of environmental factors upon the growth of the church.

First, the anti-Christian climate by itself is generally not the primary cause of decrease in the number of converts. Only when the
conditions characterizing the internal structure of the church were
highly susceptible to certain environmental factors, that particular
denomination would suffer decisive damage to the extent of its
vulnerability to such external influences. For example, the fact that
the Congregational and Presbyterian Churches had many able and
strongly nationalistic-minded students in their schools made them
more vulnerable to the rising tide of nationalism. When the loyalty
of Christians to the emperor and to their country was openly challenged, the students either quit the mission schools or transferred to

government schools. This brought about an obvious reduction in the student enrollments and partially impaired the fertile ground for conversions.

This means then that some environmental factors directly influence the conversion rate under certain circumstances. During the decade of the 1890's, there were such factors as Japan's economic crisis as well as prosperity and the government's policy of "strict enforcement" which restricted the natural flow of converts into the church by creating a crisis in mission schools or by diminishing the efficiency of the mission machine. Fortunately, none of these factors caused too much damage, because the government policy remained only for a short duration and notable decrease in enrollments was confined largely to Congregational- and Presbyterian-related schools. But, had the missionary forces been pinned down to a few treaty ports for a considerable length of time while the churches were growing outside the treaty ports in small cities and rural towns, then the effect of the government's hard line policy would have been detrimental to the increase of converts. And, had the mission schools been incapacitated and student enrollments drastically reduced, then the crisis in mission schools would have been truly crucial to the rate of growth through conversions.

Second, the various factors creating the anti-Christian climate are more the causes of membership leakage than of the declining number of converts. During the period of this chapter, the adverse environmental factors in general had more to do with encouraging membership leakage than with keeping people from coming into the church. They hardened even more the attitudes towards Christianity of the great majority of people who were tightly bound to the conservative mores of traditional Japan. The general climate, unfavorable to Christianity, explains why there were not more conversions than there actually were during the 1890's. The range of people who were responsive to Western ideology and religion was narrowed. While the pro-Western climate of the 1880's facilitated *popular* response to Christianity, the anti-Western sentiments of the following decade militated against the spread of the Christian faith. When the tide was against the things of the West, people who, under a more favorable circumstance, would adhere to them became rather cautious, especially regarding matters related to an alien religion. But as we have shown earlier, there were many conversions. Their number in each denomination was quite substantial and placed Japan as one of the more fertile mission lands. If it had not been contrasted with the high conversion rate of the late 1880's, this would have been more generally seen. Without the loss through severe membership leakage, Japanese Protestantism would have enjoyed distinct church growth despite all the socio-cultural obstacles which it encountered at that time.

The drainage of membership was the more troublesome by-product of the hardened spirit of the day. The stiffening of the attitude of the general populace against Christianity simply meant that the young Christians, converted mostly while being at school or shortly thereafter, faced stronger opposition from their families and surroundings and that many of them traveled on a fateful road towards indifference, thus soon becoming post-baptismal dropouts. It is true that no matter how oppressive anti-Christian measures and sentiments became, there were always people within the society who were religiously motivated enough, at least around the time of baptism, to make a stand for their faith. As Nida would put it,

> in general, Christianity suffers less from frontal attacks than by indirect opposition, for the blood of martyrs always attracts the strong-hearted.[66]

While many young people turned to the Christian faith being fully cognizant of possible disinheritance from their families and out of religious motives, since they came in one by one and had no family reasons for remaining Christian, they were soon drawn back into the non-Christian orbit heavily influenced by the adverse environmental factors.

Thus, the environmental factors may be said to have affected church growth in these major ways. First, these factors make it more difficult to become Christian, but usually they do not prevent conversion. The obstacle can be surmounted. Second, decrease of the conversion rate reduced the efficiency of the mission machine by chilling the church's evangelistic fervor, drastically diminishing evangelistic forces (both missionary and national), and freezing their activities. Third, these factors, under many circumstances especially those then prevalent in Japan, work against church growth by fostering membership leakage. In spite of numerous socio-cultural obstacles facing the church during this period, the Protestant movement did not lack accessions through baptisms. The unfavorable climate apparently did not discourage those who accepted Christianity. But the problem harassing this period was rather the failure of the churches to conserve existing church memberships. A large backdoor was created and kept open by various factors, some environmental, others churchly. The degree of membership leakage in each church, more than anything else, contributed to the fluctuation of its growth rate. The denominations which demonstrated notable progress, therefore, were those which had the lowest rate of membership leakage and whose internal structures were less vulnerable to the negative influence of environmental factors.

CHAPTER IV

Christian Resurgence, 1903-1918

Socio-Cultural Setting

The cold, wintry climate hostile to Christianity appeared to have eased with the dawn of a new century. The Protestant church of the 1890's was severely tested by both the external challenge and the internal crisis. Though there were denominational variations, all churches felt the harsh blow of the north wind; a few churches were less equipped to cope with it than others. For the decade and a half after the turn of the century, the church in Japan once again revealed its vitality reminiscent of the period of the 1880's. Intense evangelistic zeal characterized the period, but this time the church's massive evangelistic efforts were more carefully planned and less spontaneous. The church was now getting its major support from the newly emerged class of people in the more industrialized society of Japan. With the growth of industrialization, this particular class expanded, and the church found its strongest — if not its sole — ally in this group of people. This single-class pattern became more consolidated by 1939 and is still dominant today. The present chapter seeks to examine the phenomenon of Christian resurgence by describing and analyzing the structural changes which took place inside and outside the church during this period.

1. A changed attitude towards Christianity. While some of the components constituting the anti-Christian climate of the 1890's remained intact, there were ample evidences that the bitterness of the climate had "eased" by 1903.[1] Copeland's carefully documented study presents the following evidences. (1) The rate of Protestant advance during 1900-1919 accelerated over the accessions of the 1890's (from 42,451 communicants in 1900 to 75,608 in 1910 — an increase of about seventy-eight percent).[2] (2) The spirit of enlivened interest in Christianity was manifested by the rise in the sales of Christian literature after 1895[3] and by the increased attendance at worship services and various Christian conferences after 1896.[4] This active interest in Christianity was not found only among the existing, battered Christians from the 1890's. As the severe climate began to ameliorate, the general public also softened its hardened attitude towards Christianity, and some among them took active interest in it by reading Christian literature and being present at church services. (3) The missionary correspondence of the late 1890's contained frequent references to the turning of open enmity into indifference and further to a gradual change in the attitude of the general populace becoming more favorable towards Christianity. Thus, one Christian observer wrote in 1901: "There are plain evidences in every part of Japan that Christianity is regarded with more favour than it was a few years ago."[5] Several causes for this changed attitude may be delineated.

Some of the immediate factors bringing about the change were politico-psychological, churchly, and socio-economic.

Just as the failure of treaty revision in 1889 served as the catalyst which prompted various indigenous reactions, the success of treaty negotiations must be regarded as an influential factor. Foreign Minister Mutsu successfully concluded his negotiations with Britain in 1894 concerning extra-territoriality. Other countries followed Britain's example in the next few years. The revised treaties were ratified in 1898 and went into operation in the following year.[6] Although customs rights were not restored until 1911, the psychological effect of this long-awaited political event could not contain the joyous sentiment of the Japanese who, in turn, responded more amicably to the foreigners and their religion. Japan's self-consciousness as a member of the family of nations tipped the precarious balance between conservative and liberal tendencies among the Japanese in favor of the latter. Or, the growing conviction that Japan's isolationism was no longer tenable stayed conservative forces at least for a while.

The Sino-Japanese War of 1894-95 also helped create a salutary response towards Christianity; it provided the occasion for some Christian individuals to combat the perennial charge that Christians were unpatriotic. Christian soldiers demonstrated their courage and rendered their services for their country just as other Japanese. Christians at home devoted their energy to comfort the servicemen, both wounded and lonely. Even an organization called the *Doshikai* (Association of the Like-minded) came into being for the purpose of sending out lecturers throughout Japan to declare China's guilt and Japan's innocence in the provocation of war and to distribute Bibles and tracts among the soldiers.[7] Such acts of loyalty and helpfulness on the part of Christian individuals in wartime Japan were much appreciated.

Furthermore, the changed attitude towards Christianity was caused by the positive appraisal of Christian charity shown at the time when Japan was plagued by natural disasters. In October, 1891, Aichi and Gifu Prefectures suffered most from a series of violent earthquakes giving the death toll of 22,000 persons and leaving a million and a half homeless. Again in June of 1896, a devastating seismic wave claimed the lives of 30,000 people and demolished 2,500 houses on the northeast shores of Japan. A disaster of lesser magnitude, this time in Hokkaido, occurred in the fall of 1898 destroying many villages.[8] In all these incidents, Christians, regardless of their national origin, and the Red Cross, considered in Japan as an arm of the Christian Church, organized relief work and aided the bereaved. The manifestation of Christian charity won the hearts of many Japanese and was, no doubt, a factor in alleviating hostility towards Christianity.

Finally, the region which came under the liberal influence of more industrialized city culture grew larger by 1903. The rural region of Japan had always been the hotbed of conservatism tightly bound to traditional mores and loyalties, but with increased cultural diffusion caused by the expansion in the means of communication and transportation, the liberal influence of the city reached farther into the interior. Moreover, the structural changes which Japanese society was undergoing at that time gave birth to a new breed of men and their cohorts who, detached from the traditional *milieu,* had little need of conforming themselves to the stringencies which dictated the lives of the ordinary folks. The people of this class were freer than any group of persons in society to respond to Christianity, and inasmuch as the church monopolized them in its membership from that time on to date, we shall describe the circumstance surrounding the birth of this rising class in order to understand the nature and scope of the structural changes within society.

2. Impact of industrialization upon social structure. Japan's industrial development on a more expansive scale began in the 1890's, especially in the latter half of that decade.[9] And already by the beginning of the twentieth century, the initial phase of the industrial revolution was completed as the stage of industrial capital was replaced by that of private capital.[10] The characteristic features of Japanese capitalism were as follows. First, since the time of the Meiji Restoration, the country devoted its life to becoming a strong military power. The armament industry naturally received priority and the progress in other fields was rather nominal. Thus, the living standard of the people did not rise with increased industrial attainment. Second, capitalism in Japan advanced with the coming into power of the *zaibatsu* (financial cliques). Giant family trusts such as Mitsui, Mitsubishi, and others received strong backing from the government and served the purpose of the state. With Japan's engagement in the wars against China and Russia and in World War I, the colonial territory became enlarged and capitalism rapidly grew accompanying the development of Japanese imperialism aided by the *zaibatsu*. Third, Japanese industry was marked by the predominance of small and medium scale enterprises. The following table reveals this fact.

Table 6
Number of Factories, by Number of Workers (Percent)

	5-10	10-30	30-50	50-100	100-500	500-1000	1000+	Total
1909	16,802	10,872	2,034	1,460	980	82	58	32,228
	(52.0)	(33.4)	(6.2)	(4.5)	(3.4)	(0.3)	(0.2)	(100.0)
1914	14,655	11,553	2,342	1,803	1,155	124	85	31,717
	(46.2)	(36.4)	(7.4)	(5.7)	(3.6)	(0.4)	(0.3)	(100.0)
1919	20,118	15,648	3,466	2,474	1,881	202	160	43,949
	(45.7)	(35.6)	(7.9)	(5.6)	(4.3)	(0.5)	(0.4)	(100.0)
1924	23,415	16,405	3,540	2,585	1,953	268	227	48,394
	(48.7)	(33.8)	(7.3)	(5.3)	(4.0)	(0.6)	(0.5)	(100.0)
1929	23,187	17,287	3,917	2,831	2,170	295	200	59,887
	(55.5)	(28.9)	(6.5)	(4.7)	(3.6)	(0.5)	(0.3)	(100.0)

Source: Mikio Sumiya, *Social Impact of Industrialization in Japan* (Tokyo: Printing Bureau, Ministry of Finance, 1963), p. 114.

In 1909, factories with more than 500 workers made up 0.5 percent of 32,000. Factories with less than thirty workers amounted to as much as 85.4 percent. More than half of all factories in Japan (52 percent) employed only from five to ten people. This last statement especially is strong evidence for the small scale of Japanese industry. By 1929, this trend further increased by 3.5 percent. With the factory law being enacted as late as 1916 and the size of the average factory being as small as it was, labor conditions were bad, and much of employer-employee relationship was dominated by the feudalistic paternalism of the old family system.

Having briefly touched on Japan's industrial development and its characteristics, we shall sketch some pertinent effects of industrialization. First, industrialization helped accelerate the pace of urbanization. The increasing rate of industrial production simply meant the growth in the demand for unskilled labor and other factory workers. The second and third sons of farm families and impoverished tenant farmers moved to the city in and after the 1890's and constituted the lower strata of urban society.[11] The daughters of poor farmers also worked in various manufacturing enterprises in the city. Textile industry absorbed many such workers. According to a 1909 survey, the women workers numbered half a million, approximately sixty percent of all factory laborers.[12] These male and female workers migrated to the city in large numbers.

The phenomenon of urbanization may be further spoken of in terms of city influence over village society. Increased industrialism developed capitalistic economy, created geographic and social mobility, and expanded the means of communication and transportation. All these factors readily influenced the developed sector of the rural region to be more like a city in its style of life.

Second, industrialization together with urbanization gradually transformed the family structure in the urban region. On the basis of Teizo Toda's comparative study of rural and urban families in 1920, Masuoka concluded that "the size of the urban family varies inversely with the size of cities. It is largest in the small cities and smallest in the large urban centers."[13] Mobility and the tendency to postpone marriage will account for the diminishing size of the modern Japanese family.[14] The typical rural migrant followed the pattern of single-man migration to the city and established a nuclear family of husband and wife. Thus the segmentation of the lineage was inevitable, and the urban family generally moved in the direction of becoming more atomized. The bond between the rural stem family and the urban branch family would normally lessen, and it is highly conceivable that the newly established family in the city would enjoy considerable freedom from the traditional family system. Why most rural migrants could not enjoy this freedom will be discussed later.

Third, industrialization presupposes the emergence of various classes in society. Industrial society contains within it capitalists, industrial workers, and white-collar people. In the case of Japan, where did the constituent members of these classes come from? The prime mover of capital formation in Japan was a group of rich, landed farmers who developed various manufacturing industries. While many of these disappeared soon after 1887 due to repeated depressions in the countryside, the closing down of European markets for sericultural products, and change in the scale of industry, the most prominent of them survived and became more powerful under government patronage. However, as noted earlier, Japanese capitalism made a giant stride only as a handful of financial families established themselves as *zaibatsu* and collaborated with the state and its ambitious undertakings in rapid military build-up and aggressive colonization. Industrial magnates and high ranking bureaucrats were to be classified as capitalists.

The industrial workers came from three main sources.[15] Some of them were the ex-*samurai (shizoku)* who, after the Meiji Restoration, disintegrated as a class and were deprived of their former political, economic, and social privileges. Many of them were left with no choice but to seek employment in the factory. Others were the artisans of feudal Japan whose skills were replaced by machinery. But the largest supplier of industrial labor was the countryside. The farmers who lost their land during the depressions either became tenant farmers or migrated to the city with their families. Further, the second and third sons in farm families were the surplus population in rural society. Part of them moved to the city to be employed as industrial workers and eventually established themselves in the lower strata of urban society, but another part of them furnished the seasonal labor force in mining and construction works. During the less busy season of the year, these young farmers left their village to bring in extra income to supplement their family budget. The daughters of poor farmers also had to work and found an open market in the textile industry. It is said that the majority of women workers in textiles ranged from fifteen to twenty years old, and if those up to thirty were counted, almost ninety percent of them were young, unmarried women.[16] After working in the city for a few years, these women returned to their home village for marriage. This was the usual pattern and speaks of their conservative character despite their urban involvement. The industrial workers, then, came partly from impoverished *shizoku* and deprived artisans, but largely from the countryside. This latter source may be divided into two categories: (1) rural migrants who eventually established their home in the city and (2) seasonal and short-term laborers whose roots were heavily embedded in the village.

The third class of people to appear in Japan at the turn of the century was the group commonly known as white-collar workers. They constituted the middle class strata in society, but unlike the middle class workers were the members of the *new* middle class whose category excluded the rich farmers, the so-called intellectuals in the countryside, and the well-to-do merchants who, along with the descendants of the former *samurai,* constituted the *old* middle class. Thus, the rising middle class was made up solely of white-collar workers on salary. C. Wright Mills well describes this structural change.

> The nature and well-being of the old middle class can best be sought in the condition of entrepreneurial property; of the new middle class, in the economics and sociology of occupations. The numerical decline of the older, independent sectors of the middle class is an incident in the centralization of property; the numerical rise of the newer salaried employees is due to the industrial mechanics by which the occupations composing the new middle class have arisen.[17]

Education was the factor which enabled social mobility, so the role of education must not be overlooked in the development of the new middle class. To meet the demands of qualified manpower in industry and administrative systems, the Japanese government quickly improved its educational scheme extending compulsory education from three to four years in 1900 and from four to six in 1908. Besides, compulsory education was offered free of charge and the enrollment rose to ninety and later to ninety-five percent.[18] Secondary education facilities were likewise improved, and the number of students in higher education climbed rapidly within the period of this book, as is evident from the following table.

Table 7
Students in Middle and Higher Schools

Year	Middle School Boys	Middle School Girls	High School	College
1889	11,530	3,274	14,233	774
1902	95,027	21,523	27,647	4,046
1912	128,973	64,871	40,530	8,946
1921	194,416	154,470	62,499	26,208
1930	345,691	341,574	110,594	69,605
1940	432,288	518,584	161,761	81,999

Source: Kirisutokyo Gakko Domei, *Nihon-ni Okeru Kirisutokyo Gakko Kyoiku-no Genjo* (Tokyo: The Education Association of Christian Schools in Japan, 1961), pp. 7, 14, 20.

Those who received middle and higher education were the potential candidates for the white-collar class. Rich, landed farmers and small scale entrepreneurs were anxious to send their children to obtain higher education to assure them of a place in the new salaried and managerial class.[19] In spite of rapid increase in the number of students during the first four decades of this century, the road leading to the new status class was considerably narrow. For instance, 260,000 persons, only 1.1 percent of Japan's productive age population, were graduates of middle and high schools in 1905.[20] Therefore, those who belonged to this clsss were the elite within the Japanese society.

Ecclesiastical Setting

The structural changes of the society, on which we have thus far elaborated, had significant bearing on the changes which occurred within the church. By the end of this period, the Protestant constituency shifted from the *old* middle class to the *new* and from male predominance to female. The church's approach to evangelism was now less spontaneous and more structured than the previous decades. More people in Japan heard and "responded" to the gospel. In terms of growth, all denominations except the Disciples grew substantially after the cold spell of the 1890's. The gulf separating the fast and slow growing churches became evident by 1918 and more pronounced by 1939. For the sake of convenience, we shall call the top four churches the "expansionists" and the bottom four the "slow growers." The old problem of membership loss, too, was affected by these structural changes. While some of the previous causes were discarded for being no longer viable, others stubbornly persisted and, if anything, were reinforced by these changes. The fact that these changes did take place must now be established before we proceed to our growth analysis.

1. Structural changes within the church constituency. Pieters, in his 1909 study of mission problems, mentioned the large proportion of urban, white-collar workers within the church membership. It was pointed out that the artisan, merchant, and farming classes were almost untouched by the gospel and yet, they comprised nine-tenths of Japan's total population. Furthermore, he noted the almost "hopeless" case of the agricultural people.[21]

In the 1922 issue of *The International Review of Missions,* Fisher reported the following:

> An analysis of the membership drawn from different classes, in the United Brethren Church, shows that 30 percent were in commercial pursuits, 28 percent students, 8 percent government officials and soldiers, 6 percent nurses and doctors, 3 percent artists, and 28 percent unclassified.[22]

While recognizing that these percentages of the United Brethren Church would not apply equally to other churches, the author was of the firm conviction that the Protestant church in Japan was generally composed of the educated classes in cities and towns and that the farmers, artisans, and manual laborers were barely represented.[23]

More recently, Jaeckel offered the following facts for 1953: farmers constituted 50 percent of Japan's total population, laborers 27 percent, fishermen 3 percent, and middle class/intelligentsia 20 percent. In like manner, farmers comprised 2 percent of Japan's Christians, laborers 3 percent, fishermen .05 percent, and middle class/intelligentsia 94.05 percent.[24]

From these statistics, it seems fair to conclude that Protestantism in Japan was largely made up of the white-collar workers since the turn of the century. Or, to put it negatively, Christianity, for various reasons, could not penetrate into any other strata of society except the white-collar class.

The shift from male to female predominance was another aspect of the church's structural change. Ikado dates this shift to have occurred since the Taisho period (1912-26) and says that the ratio of women to men in Protestant churches in 1956 was six to four.[25] The writer's own study of "Ten Kyodan Churches in Kyoto"[26] conducted in 1969 confirms this point. There are these possible reasons for the female predominance. First, the mission boards emphasized female education, and a large number of female students became converted after 1900. With the changed attitude towards the West, there was a noticeable reaction favoring female education which "redounded to the advantage of the Christian girls' schools."[27] Second, the emancipation of urban females was gradually taking place due to the increased cultural diffusion, the atomization of the family, and the spread of female education not only on the elementary but also on the secondary level. More females, though extremely limited in number, were able to enjoy freedom and individuation in large cities. Third, wives of white-collar workers could respond to the gospel with less difficulty than any other group of females in the Japanese society. Thus, a larger percentage of the female population was relatively free to accept the Christian faith, and a considerable number actually did.

2. Notable growth features. There are two points which we need to specify. First, the substantial growth of communicants was registered in all churches except in the Disciples of Christ which netted only eight for 1903-1917. The top four churches, shown on Figure 1 (p. 6), increased as follows for the priod of a decade and a half: Presbyterian by 21,000, Congregational by 11,000, Methodist by 17,000, and Episcopal by 5,000. The American Baptist, Southern Baptist, and Seventh-Day Adventist Churches also revealed substantial growth, though the evidence on the graph was less conspicuous.[28]

Second, we simply raise the question regarding the growth feature already mentioned. From 1903 to 1939 the graph indicates two major trends: the trend of so-called expansionists and that of slow growers. How are we to explain the ever widening gulf between the four fast growing churches at the top and the four slow growing churches at the bottom?

3. Mass evangelistic campaigns and denominational efforts. One outstanding characteristic of the Protestant movement in Japan after 1900 would be the aggressive evangelistic campaigns conducted by various denominations both jointly and individually.

During the first eighteen years of this century, there were a few significant cooperative ventures. The Third General Conference of Protestant Missionaries held in 1900 resolved to enter the new century with a renewed emphasis on evangelism. The national churches which had gone through the period of spiritual depression in the 1890's were keenly aware of the need to revitalize their life and to proclaim the faith in the wake of a new century. The convergence of these concerns issued in a nationwide evangelistic campaign of 1901-1902. It was called "The Twentieth Century Grand Evangelical Movement" *(Taikyo Dendo)* and was described by Iglehart as follows:

> The campaign included series of mass rallies in the larger cities, visiting teams for single meetings in the smaller places, evangelistic appeals, the signing of [decision] cards, after-meetings for personal work, and the final follow-up assumed by local pastors.[29]

This method of evangelism was highly structured with careful planning in contrast to the previously known method whereby spiritually sensitive Christian individuals spontaneously witnessed their faith to relatives and friends. Teams of well-known pastors, theologians, and Christian scholars were sent to big and medium-sized cities to conduct mass rallies. Lectures given by these men of distinction appealed primarily to the intellectual class in the Japanese society largely made up of white-collar workers and students. Thus, the campaign was successful among the new middle class intellectuals residing in large cities.[30] During 1901 those who attended the meetings numbered 322,245, those who signed decision cards 15,440, and those who received baptism 1,181.[31] By September, 1902 when the campaign ended, nearly 20,000 persons had signed their names as inquirers.[32]

At the Osaka Exposition of 1903, several large Protestant denominations banded together to maintain the "Christian Union Evangelical Hall" where hymns were sung, sermons preached, and instructions concerning Christianity given for fully five months beginning March 1st. Over sixteen thousand persons out of 246,000 who attended the meetings signed their decision cards.[33]

Another cooperative venture was the National Evangelistic Campaign *(Zenkoku Kyodo Dendo)* which was carried on from 1914 to 1917. The results were as follows: 3,472 meetings, 642,555 persons who attended them, and 21,415 inquirers.[34]

It is necessary at this point to comment on the nature of response which the Protestant movement in Japan had been getting through these and ensuing mass evangelistic campaigns. In all these meetings, a huge number of people gathered and listened to the sermons and addresses given by prominent ministers and educators. A considerable number "responded" by signing decision cards, though some among them were already church members.[35] Many who did so, however, did not realize that they were taking a serious step and saw little need of attaching themselves to a Christian church for further instruction.[36] Yet there were those who made serious decisions. Unlike the feudal days, more individuals in modern Japan were able to enjoy the privilege of making many independent decisions. "But," says Iglehart, "of all relationships religious affiliation was the least private and the most strongly communal."[37] Therefore,

> multitudes of people, mostly young persons and students in a genuine spiritual response signed cards of decision but only rarely could one muster enough courage to go on to a final commitment.[38]

Thus, only a fraction of those who "responded" went so far as to be baptized.

Perhaps, part of the problem, as McKenzie pointed out, was that

> no effective means had been provided for getting the new inquirers at once into intimate relations with the pastors and other Christian workers. Consequently, a larger proportion of those who made a start in the meetings just drifted away, and when later on they were invited to the churches through a printed notice, or searched for by visiting committees or pastors, they did not respond or could not be found.[39]

It may be concluded that the mass campaigns in general served to create the climate favorable to Christianity as evidenced by a considerably large number of respondents. But it was also a fact that only a minute fraction of them actually fed into church membership.

Not only were there nation-wide, interdenominational mass campaigns, but also there were many denominational evangelistic activities in conjunction with or between these cooperative ventures. Indeed, it is no exaggeration to speak of the post-1900 period until the end of this book as that of intense evangelistic campaigns. These forward drives were called by various names such as "Concentration Evangelism" (Shuchu Dendo), "Extension Evangelism" (Kakucho Dendo), and "Special Evangelism" (Tokubetsu Dendo). Churches conducted numerous campaigns in honor of mission anniversaries. Similar tactics with some variations characterized these evangelistic efforts. The "Concentration Evangelism" of the Congregational Church held in 1907 may illustrate the procedure.

> A certain center is selected where there is already a growing church. This field is diligently cultivated for a period of some months by the local workers, getting the Christians ready for the new advance, Bible instruction both within and without the church. Then a number of

pastors of note and experience from the metropolitan centers come in, and for a period of from a week to two weeks carry on a vigorous evangelistic campaign, with nightly platform meetings and daily Bible instruction and personal interviews.[40]

The follow-ups were more manageable in this type of campaign than the mass rally.

4. Membership leakage continues. That all churches suffered from huge membership loss has been specified in Chapter III. Now it needs to be noted that a similar problem existed for the period under review. Some churches, however, greatly lessened the percentage of leakage as is shown below.

Table 8
Decadal Membership Leakage, 1906-1915

Church	Decadal baptismal total	Membership gain for the decade	Decadal loss	Percentage of leakage (%)
Episcopala	9,383	3,021	6,362	68
Presbyterian	19,570	16,485	3,085	16
A. Baptist	3,773	2,182	1,591	42
Congregationalb	15,312	8,556	6,756	44
Methodist	13,536	4,575	8,961	66
Disciples	1,957	107	1,850	95
S. Baptist	648	470	178	27

a. The figures are for the decade, 1908-1917.

b. For the decade, 1907-1916.

Source: Compiled from *The Christian Movement in Japan* (1907-1918). The baptismal figures for American and Southern Baptist Churches were taken from their annual reports. See American Baptist Foreign Mission Society, *Annual Reports,* 1907-1916 (Boston: Foreign Mission Rooms) and Southern Baptist Convention, *Annual of the Southern Baptist Convention,* 1907-1916 (Atlanta, Ga.: The Franklin Printing and Publishing Co.).

The Presbyterian Church, for example, registered the total of 19,570 baptisms during 1906-1915 with an average of 2,000 baptisms per year. The communicant membership climbed from 15,076 in 1905 to 31,561 in 1915 — a decadal increase of 16,485. Had the church retained all the additions through baptism (not even counting the transfers from another denomination), its membership would have been 34,646 in 1915 or 3,085 more than what the church actually registered for the same year. This simply means that the church lost sixteen percent of the number baptized during the decade. It must be made clear, however, that many of those lost may have been Christians for several years and that those who disappeared from the church in any given year were not necessarily the newly baptized for that year. Contrasted from the eighty-four percent annual average rate of leakage for 1890-1902, the Presbyterian

Church during this decade made a remarkable improvement in the retention of its membership.

The Southern Baptist Church also kept a high retention rate, but the rest[41] of the churches continued to be plagued by a considerably high rate of membership loss. The Disciples of Christ with ninety-five percent leakage understandably could not grow. How should we interpret the phenomenon of continued membership loss? We might note that while the environmental causes unique to the period of the 1890's no longer had a binding effect on the leakage, most causes internal to the church continued to exist, especially those relating to the physical and intellectual mobility of the membership constituency, the marriage pattern, and familial relations.[42] Ikado reported that the shift from male predominance to female occurred since the Taisho period. This structural change within the church made the Protestant constituency more vulnerable to membership leakage; young Christian women before World War II faced more difficult times to keep their faith alive than young men. Thus, in this period as in the one before, the problem of a backdoor constituted one prime factor in reducing the growth rate of most churches.

Church Growth Interpretation

The preceding sections described the structural changes which occurred within the society around the turn of the century and their effects upon the structure of the church. And we noted that in the midst of these changes all churches except the Disciples grew remarkably. This section aims at first analyzing the general trend of resurgent growth which most churches exhibited during this period, then making clear the reasons why only a narrow strip of population actually accepted the Christian faith, and finally explaining the gulf which set in between expansionists and slow growers. The following questions, if answered correctly, will illumine our understanding of Japanese church growth for the early decades of this century.

1. Why did the phenomenon of Christian resurgence take place? McGavran, after critically studying the various mission fields of the world, concluded that the church would normally grow when "environmental and church factors favorable to growth appeared at the same time."[43] This may very well be the case in the resurgent growth of post-1900 Japan.

Environmentally speaking, the bitter climate of the 1890's eased by 1903, and the church faced a less hostile and increasingly

amicable attitude of the general populace. This change in attitude
was brought about by the success of treaty negotiations, the patriotic
service of Christians during the Sino-Japanese War, the positive
appraisal of Christian charity rendered at the time of natural disasters, and the extension of city culture into the interior. This changed
attitude contributed towards making a potentially responsive segment of society manifestly responsive. The students, while generally
more sensitive to the Christian claim, became hesitant under the
anti-Christian climate of the 1890's. But, when the cold spell began
to ameliorate, their responsive nature once again returned to their
property.

Besides the improved attitude of the people towards Christianity,
there was a general swell of the population most responsive to the
Christian faith. Japan's rapid industrialization created the white-
collar class whose dominant occupation characterized the Protestant constituency since the beginning of this century. Why particularly this class was receptive to Christianity more than any other
segment of sqciety will be discussed momentarily. Here we simply
indicate that this class grew larger as the improved government
facilities turned out a much greater number of graduates from
middle and higher schools. Graduates from these and private institutions of similar grades were the potential candidates for this
class. Table 7 (p. 93) clearly portrays the rapid increase of the
student population. Industrialization thus caused the expansion of
the white-collar workers and their successors. Further, there were
other contributing factors such as increasing education of Japanese
in the West, the effects of World War I, and the desire to emulate the
West.

Given these environmental factors, the churches after 1900 conducted aggressive denominational and interdenominational
evangelistic campaigns. The missionaries and the national leaders
shared the burning passion for the conversion of the entire nation.
Yet their efforts in these campaigns, according to Best,[44] were di-
rected to the rising white-collar class and students. "It had taken the
church a decade," continues the author, "to realize what was
happening but she was quick to see where her new opportunities
lay."[45] Judging from the white-collar predominance of the Protestant constituency during this period, the churches unquestionably
took full advantage of the opportunities afforded them. Perhaps, the

churches may not have consciously aimed at any specific segment of society at first, but indeed those who actively responded were from the narrowly confined stratum. The unusual receptivity of this group and the hard-shell character of others dictated the gradual concentration of the church's effort upon this limited margin of population thereafter. The phenomenon of resurgent growth may thus be interpreted by the combination of two elements: the emergence and growth of white-collar workers and the aggressive evangelistic efforts poured out on them. The Protestant movement in general saturated its evangelistic energy on the most receptive portion of Japan's population and was rewarded with good results.

2. Why did the church grow almost exclusively among the white-collar class? Before analyzing the white-collar receptivity, we shall first examine why Christianity could not penetrate into other sectors of society.

By far the largest single class of people in Japan during this period was the farming population. Whatever success Protestantism had with this group was limited to about a ten-year span between 1877 and 1887. For various reasons,[46] the rural church gradually lost its strength after 1887 and, by the turn of the century, became virtually squeezed out of the village society. Due to the restrictions of family and hamlet[47] reinforced by the emperor institution, the rural population remained conservative throughout the period of this book.

The church, too, did not make serious attempts to reach this population after 1900. On the premise that "Old Japan" would soon disintegrate, the church paid its secondary attention to rural areas.[48] It is said that no more than ten percent of the total Protestant missionary force was assigned to full time rural work in the twenties and that only seventy-nine American and European missionaries (6.4 percent of the total force) resided in towns with a population of less than 25,000 people in 1922.[49] Furthermore, about one hundred missionaries out of 1,200 were in the country areas according to Butterfield's estimate of 1931.[50] Only a handful of them, however, were to be rightly called rural missionaries in terms of their preparation. When the church did act after Butterfield's visit to Japan, it

> found that the thought life and values of farming people severely impeded [its] . . . efforts. The conservatism of rural people, particularly their suspicion of everything un-Japanese, was the major obstacle.[51]

Thus, Christianity was practically sealed off from the farming people due to their hardened conservatism and the urban concentration of the church's energy through structured programs.

It is also true that despite its urban onslaught through vigorous evangelistic campaigns, the church could not reach the capitalist and labor classes to any significant degree. While we discovered some references regarding the upper class receptivity during the 1880's, such entries were rarely found after 1900 in journals, missionary correspondence, and books; Christianity was a seed fallen on hard ground as far as the industrial magnates and high-ranking government officials were concerned. They were the people who, for the sake of national interest, enforced the traditional mores of Japan.

Neither did the labor class prove to be promising. The church in Japan had never been able to reach this group effectively throughout its entire history. Why was this so? Perhaps, this was due primarily to the very nature of the labor force at least for the early stage of its formation. There were, to be sure, impoverished *shizoku* and deprived artisans, but they were few compared with the farm surplus population which entered the labor market as the industrial development progressed. One type of rural supply was the migrants who eventually established their home in the city but they could not rid themselves of their rural upbringing. They were immersed in the traditional views and loyalties. The management could easily elicit from these employees similar response as the head of the family received from the rest of the members. Paternalism characterized this relationship. Such a paternalistic relationship was intensified by the small scale of Japanese industry. Sumiya stated that even

> big business . . . used traditional thought patterns as a way to harmonize conflict between laborers and employers, and tried to establish a family-like principle of management.[52]

The other type of rural supply was the seasonal and short-term laborers. During the less busy seasons, the countryside suffered the overflow of labor, and the bodily able young men sought employment in mining and construction works. There was also an outlet for excess female labor. It became almost customary for the daughters of poor farmers to spend the better portion of their teens in the textile mills and other places of work. These laborers, by virtue of their inevitable return to the countryside, remained solidly "country-minded" and were "rooted in traditions of respectful deference to the authorities and to the employer."[53] Acceptance of Christianity was hardly conceivable by these who were docile and intended to go back to the social *milieu* antithetical to Christianity.

In short, the awakening of an individual consciousness was slow to develop among the labor class and Christianity found it difficult to penetrate into it.

Why particularly, then, was the white-collar class more receptive to the Christian faith? In asking this question, it is well for us to keep in mind the receptivity of students since they were the soon-to-be white-collar workers.

First, the white-collar people were the most mobile population within the society and were free of old traditions and social relations.[54] They were least bound by the feudalistic restrictions.

Second, most of those who belonged to this class absorbed new ideas of all kinds from abroad in the process of acquiring new techniques necessary for industrialization. So Christianity often appealed to them. And the bureaucrats were less inclined to oppress this class because they needed its help.[55] Thus, the white-collar people enjoyed a degree of freedom which was denied to the farming and labor classes.

Third, caught by the competitiveness of the capitalistic system, the white-collar people were thrown into a race to constantly improve their status by acquiring economic security and obtaining power.[56] Yet power hunger was never satisfied because there was always a step above to aim for and consequently many of them experienced *anomie* and a feeling of insecurity and void which drove them to yearn for acceptance and a group reference. A considerable number found a spiritual resting place in the church.

Fourth, in various evangelistic thrusts made after 1900, the church utilized famous figures in educational and ecclesiastical circles as speakers and evangelists. The messages delivered by them and the general tone of the meetings were highly intellectual.[57] While this intellectualism appealed to the white-collar people and students, it prevented the non-intellectual classes of the society from accepting the Christian faith.

Fifth, in a more practical vein, only the white-collar people and students had time to join the church and participate in its activities. The farmers and industrial workers were tightly restricted in their use of time due to unfavorable labor conditions.

Sixth, the white-collar people were the most awakened in

Japanese society in their individual consciousness. This was not unique to Japan, however, as it is pointed out below:

> Euro-American students of society generally agree that an outstanding characteristic correlated to the rise of modern industrial-urban phenomena has been the emergence of the importance of the individual.[58]

Since entry into the white-collar class was through higher education, the class constituents were duly exposed to the Western ideology and were intellectually most emancipated. And yet, at every turn, they were keenly made aware that collectivity orientations still overruled self-orientations throughout the period of this book and even today. As Brown stated, "the *ie* (house) is . . . the archetype of the solid, 'in-group' structure of Japanese society."[59] This means that the group is more important than the individual. In the words of Matsumoto,

> collectivity orientations remain predominant in the family, in occupational ties, in labor unions, in village life, and in politics. Where attitudinal changes are occurring, they are shifting from the collectivity orientations based on hierarchical doctrines, paternal authoritarianism, and lineal ancestry toward collectivity orientations based on collateral ties, peer-groups, and egalitarian views.[60]

While more freedom is given to the individual today, the white-collar people before World War II suffered "frustration of the ego"[61] in all cases when encountering the dominant note of collectivity emphasis along the traditional family ideology. Thus, both the awakening of the individual consciousness and frustration of the ego made part of the white-collar people most sensitive and responsive to the Christian faith.

    3. What contributed to the widening of the gulf[62] between expansionists and slow growers? By 1918 one group of churches grew more substantially in actual communicant membership than the other group, seemingly creating a gulf between them. The gulf became further widened by 1939; the growth lines of expansionists on Figure 1 (p. 6) are shooting upward while those of slow growers crawl along the chronological scale. There are at least six reasons for this phenomenon.

First, the expansionists from 1901 to 1939 had a far greater number of missionaries and ordained nationals than the slow growers, though some slow growers actually registered greater percentage gains than expansionists within the given period. Table 9 given below reveals these facts. The peak of the missionary force of each denomination is said to have been around 1924.[63] And as the missionary force declined, the expansionists countered the situation by training many more national pastors. The slow growers also showed a rising trend, but their increase in actual number rather than percentage growth was very minimal.

Table 9
Missionaries[a] and Ordained Nationals, 1901-1939

	1901		1920		1939	
Church	Missionaries	Nationals	Missionaries	Nationals	Missionaries	Nationals
(Expansionists)						
Presbyterian	153	60	215	178	156	337
Methodist	147	101	221		178	325
Congregational	71	70	65	67	43	126
Episcopal	224	50	228	122	133	260
(Slow Growers)						
A. Baptist	56	8	73	24	25	33
S. Baptist	12	0	19	10	14	12
Disciples	20	9	33	21	5	23
S.D.A.			5	8	29	16

a. Missionary figures include wives.

Source: Compiled from The Japan Christian Year Books (1903, 1921, 1940); Seventh-Day Adventists, Annual Statistical Reports of the General Conference of Seventh-Day Adventists (1921, 1940).

In fact, all the national forces of the slow growers put together amounted to far less than the number raised by the Congregational Church which had the least number of ordained ministers among the expansionists.

The progress of slow growers was hampered by much shuffling of missionary personnel due to illness, death, furlough, retirement, and transfer. The newly arrived missionaries had little chance of working with experienced colleagues. There were also many missionary dropouts on account of discouragement. Furthermore, the lean national force thinly scattered did not contribute to growth.

Second, the expansionists organized more churches and increased the number of contacts with people. The following table reveals the growth of organized churches.

Table 10
Organized Churches, 1901-1939

Church	1901	1920	1939
(Expansionists)			
Presbyterian	71	244	359
Methodist	119	145	270
Congregational	81	152	196
Episcopal	69	195	257
(Slow Growers)			
A. Baptist	30	33	65
S. Baptist	3	12	22
Disciples	14	24	21
S.D.A.	1	9	25

Source: Compiled from *The Japan Christian Year Books* (1903, 1921, 1940).

With everything else being equal, the fisherman with ten fishing poles would normally do better than the man with one. Each of the expansionists had a much greater number of organized churches than any of the slow growers.

Third, the expansionists raised a more able and highly educated ministry and were more equipped to reach the intellectuals within society who proved to be most receptive to the Christian faith. The slow growers on the other hand suffered from lack of able leadership among the nationals.[65]

Fourth, the expansionists developed a more centralized national organization and were able to carry out comprehensive programs of evangelism. Due to their late arrival, most slow growers were continuously engaged in exploratory ventures and were slow to carve out fruitful strategies.

Fifth, the expansionists had gone through the mission-church conflict around the turn of the century and their national leaders soon realized that the work of evangelism was theirs.[66] Along with the principles of self-government and self-support, the expansionists strove for self-propagation. The zeal for evangelism, therefore, was extremely high. In contrast, the slow growers generally depended heavily upon missionaries and foreign funds. The keen awareness of "our mission" did not emerge until later.

Sixth, the expansionists emphasized the educational policy from the beginning and had better educational facilities and greater student enrollments than the slow growers. The following table shows the number of students enrolled in the denominational schools. The middle school was for males between the ages of twelve and eighteen. The girls in similar age brackets attended the high schools for girls. Here, for the sake of convenience, we have grouped both males and females together under one category combining both the middle school and college students. The purpose is to compare the enrollments between expansionists and slow growers since those in these age brackets were most responsive to the Christian faith.

Table 11
Middle School and College Students

Church	1901	1920	1939
(Expansionists)			
Presbyterian	1,261	4,090	5,079
Methodist	2,319	4,357	8,151
Congregational	895	3,579	5,456
Episcopal	419	3,323	
(Slow Growers)			
A. Baptist	320	752	2,956
S. Baptist	0	250	1,795
Disciples		477a	1,271
S.D.A.	0	35b	110c

a. The 1925 figure.
b. The 1925 figure.
c. The 1936 figure.

Source: Compiled from The Japan Christian Year Books (1903, 1921, 1927, 1937, 1940).

The slow growers generally followed the single line of direct evangelism at first but soon realized the need of establishing educational institutions. Since they were late in starting their schools, they had many less student enrollments than the expansionists. This factor contributed to the widening of the gulf because the churches with the better developed educational institutions had greater chance of accessions. The report of the commission investigating the status of mission schools supports the thesis that the influence of Christian schools was a factor in the spread of the Christian faith. On the basis of the study made for 1926-1930, the commission reported that

> the average of the graduates who were Christians was in the universities eighteen percent, in the men's colleges twenty-six percent, in the women's colleges sixty-nine, in the middle school for boys thirty, and in the high schools for girls forty-nine percent. The percentage in some schools is very low. In others it runs to nearly one hundred. When it is remembered that practically none of these students were Christians when they entered, the results by this test would seem to be highly statisfactory . . . One of the largest denominations in Japan reports that forty-six percent of all its annual baptisms are of students in its schools.[67]

There is little doubt that the mission school was definitely a power-ful evangelistic arm of the church. For example, the American Baptist Church which was late in starting its educational institutions drew a large percentage of its annual membership gain from its schools. Table 12 given below aptly illustrates this. The ten year average of additions from schools was 37.4 percent. This means that approximately thirty-seven out of every one hundred persons bap-tized in any given year were

Table 12
Percentage of School Additions
to Adult Baptisms

Year	Adult Baptisms	Added from Schools	Percentage of School Additions (%)
1928	357	119	33.3
1929	237	84	35.8
1930	333	65	17.6
1931	249	73	29.3
1932	218	75	34.4
1933	217	73	33.6
1934	178	101	56.7
1935	211	117	55.4
1936	153	59	38.5
1937	196	76	38.7

Source: Compiled from American Baptist Foreign Mission Society, *Annual Reports,* 1929-1938 (Boston: Foreign Mission Rooms).

from the mission schools. The mission school was thus a highly effective feeder into church membership.

In this chapter, we endeavored to describe and analyze the phenomena crucial to our understanding of church growth for the early decades of this century. The chapter that follows will add further insights towards the conceptualization of church growth in Japan.

CHAPTER V

Between the Wars, 1919-1939

Socio-Cultural Setting

From the church growth point of view, the period between the two world wars offers close parallels as well as a sharp contrast to other epochs in Japanese church history. During this period, the eight churches studied in this book exhibited a pattern of growth similar to that discussed in Chapter IV. Expansionists and slow growers continued to draw apart from each other and the gulf between them was further widened by 1939. Explanations of this phenomenon have already been given. Further, just as the pro-Westernism of the 1880's was met with the anti-Westernism of the following decade, the rise of the military and ultranationalism of the 1930's chilled the recurrent pro-Western fever of the 1920's. Like that of the 1890's, the period of the 1930's was said to have been difficult for church growth, but again two similar conclusions can be drawn. First, despite environmental hindrances, the church recorded substantial gains through baptisms. Second, judging from such gains, the church obviously suffered considerable membership loss, the perennial problem dealt with in Chapters III and IV.

Yet, something unusual happened in this period. As it was reported, "there has been a rapid advance in the growth of the indigenous and independent Holiness Movement."[1] Though this book concerns only the eight churches in Japan before 1900, the investigation of Japanese church growth would be incomplete were we to ignore the puzzle presented by the Holiness advance. What we see here is a conversion approach pattern of church growth in sharp contradistinction to a school approach pattern of the eight churches. This chapter attempts to examine and compare these two distinct patterns of growth.

1. The second period of westernization. From Perry to World War II Japan passed through two eras of intense westernization. The first such period was that of the 1880's and is described in Chapter II. The decade of the 1920's may be called its second. There are several possible reasons which could explain why Japan, especially in this decade, appropriated Western ideologies and style of life as readily as it did.

First, the victory of democracy over authoritarianism in World War I gave great impetus to the furtherance of democratic ideals in Japan. The Japanese witnessed before their eyes the triumph of the war waged in order to assure the safety of democracy and the collapse of authoritarian states such as the German, Austro-Hungarian, and Russian Empires.[2] Nothing was more convincing to the Japanese than the lesson taught by history that democracy was the power behind the success of the Western nations.

Second, internationalism became the national ideology. The Paris Peace Conference of 1919 accorded Japan a seat in the Council of the League of Nations, and this fact implanted in the hearts of the Japanese a keen world consciousness. Japan now took an active part in major world conferences. At Washington in the winter of 1921-1922, Japan along with Western nations recognized the territorial integrity of China and at Geneva in 1927 signed the Pact of Paris for "the renunciation of war as an instrument of national policy." Despite opposition from the military, the Japanese government agreed to the decision of the London Disarmament Conference in 1930.[3] The power politics within the government, at least until this time, was cast in favor of democracy and internationalism.

Third, the full-fledged development of the urban white-collar class meant an increase of population most susceptive to Western ideologies.⁴ Japan's industrialization advanced more rapidly during World War I. Shipments of Japanese good were suddenly in demand by countries which had traded largely with European nations whose production was now dominated by the war. An increasing number of professionals, highly trained civil and military bureaucrats, and managerial personnel were needed. Government's improved educational facilities quickly turned out such persons in large numbers who entered this privileged class. These

> urban intellectuals and white-collar workers found that education had opened for them the doors to the outside world, and they happily rushed out to bask in the light of a common world culture.⁵

The mood of the day was profound pro-Westernism.

Fourth, a turnover of government leadership to a new generation brought about the liberalization of political views and increased international cooperation. The *genro* (elder statesmen) who had been in control since the Restoration had died by the 1920's, and those who replaced them had been brought up in the liberal, democratic ideas of the West.⁶ Many of them were actually devoted to these ideas and endeavored to express them through public office.

Fifth, aspects of Western culture greatly penetrated into the urban population with the development of mass media. It is said that even

> the common people in the cities were being influenced by the outside world, not only in such externals as clothing, but also in the realm of ideas through the newspaper, literature, radio, and motion pictures.⁷

No doubt mass media reached people beyond the city walls, but they were less free than the city folks to entertain Western ideologies due to restrictions of the traditional *milieu*. The people in the city were allowed to flirt with the things of the West when the West was the model for the life style and ideology of the day. Once the Western fever subsided, only a narrow margin of the city population — namely, the intellectuals and white-collar workers — was relatively free to cherish the noble traits of Western culture such as individual freedom.

Once again as it was the experience of the 1880's, the period of the 1920's with its intense westernization afforded a greater number of people, mainly in the cities, the opportunity to fraternize with Western ideas and modes of life. However, only a small segment of society was actually free enough from external pressures to retain the spirit of democracy and internationalism with the diminishing of the Western fad. Christianity, at least for the moment, enjoyed an eager and receptive audience.

2. The rise of the military and ultranationalism. The decade that followed the liberal years of the 1920's was one of ultranationalism. While there were many proponents of ultranationalist thought in the 1920's,[8] their influence was limited because of the popularity of the West. Yet the conservative force was gaining strength to counter the desecration of traditional values. The onrush of Western culture did not come without the accompaniment of some undesirable traits often resulting from the abuse of Western ideologies and customs. Japan's rural residents abhorred the immoral practices of the city dwellers. The passage of the Oriental Exclusion Act of 1924 in the United States Congress dealt a hard blow to growing internationalism in Japan. The instability of daily life in the late 1920's created distrust of capitalism in favor of socialism,[9] and democracy was judged by some as being inadequate. Thus, "resentment against this libertinism helped to bring about the sudden rise to power of the military in the thirties."[10] From the Manchurian Incident of 1931, the militarists began to control the affairs of Japan. Cogswell describes the situation in these words:

> By building up an elaborate state cult of Shinto, centering around the person of the emperor, and by indoctrinating its youth with devotion to the emperor and blind faith in all statements said to represent his will, they secured for themselves the unquestioning loyalty and obedience of the people.[11]

The government engineered skillful programs of indoctrination through its educational institutions and of checking any undesirable movement against the vested interest of the ruling class. Especially after 1937 — with the establishment of the Konoe Cabinet and Japan's engagement in the war with China, fascism and ultranationalism became the food and breath of Japan. Under these circumstances, it is natural that Christianity faced a tremendous hurdle. An inkling of such difficulty may be seen in the following statement by McGovern.

> Between 1931 and 1941 Japan closed its doors on western ideologies; and Christianity, during these years, entered its most trying period in Japanese history . . . The Japanese Government, private patriotic organizations, and public opinion placed great pressure on the small Christian community to accommodate its thought to the nationalism in Japan.[12]

Christians in Japan were once again put on the defensive with a burden to prove their reliability rather than liability towards the national goals.

In this section we have briefly sketched two distinct periods: one, receptivity to Western ideologies similar to the pro-Westernism of the 1880's, and two, repulsion to these ideals as experienced in the 1890's.

Ecclesiastical Setting

By unraveling the puzzle of the Holiness advance, the present chapter aims at depicting more clearly the pattern of growth characterizing the eight churches. Therefore, a brief historical sketch of the Holiness Church properly belongs here. But first, we shall make a few observations as to how the eight churches responded to the circumstances of receptivity and repulsion which made up the texture of the two decades under study.

1. The state of the eight churches. All eight churches grew remarkably during the period of receptivity (1919-1930). Over the eleven year span, the Presbyterian Church increased roughly by 13,000, the Methodist by 15,000, the Congregational by 8,000, the Episcopal by 4,000, the American Baptist by 1,000, the Southern Baptist by 1,500, the Disciples by 800, and the Seventh-Day Adventist by 500. This picture of church growth somewhat changed when Christianity "entered its most trying period." The Congregational line of growth after 1930 plateaued.[13] The American Baptist Church after 1930 declined. The Southern Baptist Church entered the period of turbulence after 1932 with frequent ups and downs in its membership figures. And the Disciples stagnated after 1936. The causes for each of these situations must be scrutinized by church historians and missionary scholars who are well versed in the activities of the church during this period. Their considered judgments as to the causes of growth or decline will add immensely to the science of mission.[14] What must be emphasized at this point, however, is not that these churches succumbed to external pressures but that others overcame them. The Presbyterian, Methodist,[15] Episcopal, and Seventh-Day Adventist Churches continued to grow even after 1935. The growth of the first three churches are accounted for in our discussion of the growth of the expansionists in Chapter IV. But how do we explain the progress of the Seventh-Day

Adventist Church? Perhaps, it was largely due to its improved mission machines.[16] Further emphasis should be placed on the fact that despite adverse environment, all eight churches scored definite gains through baptism during 1929-1939 though somewhat reduced from the previous decade. The following table will show the trend of baptismal gains during the period of repulsion.

Table 13
Adult Baptisms, 1929-1939

Church	1929	1931	1933	1935	1937	1939
Presbyterian	2,691	2,554	2,697	2,507	2,355	1,929
Methodist	1,036	2,160	1,996	1,806	2,080	1,630
Congregational	1,228	4,295	1,155	858	1,038	681
Episcopal	1,412	1,170	1,344	1,007	1,093	728
A. Baptist	237	249	217	211	196	164
S. Baptist	140	130	121	146	128	117
Disciples	168		81	108	66	38
S.D.A.	77	100	115	115	133	69

Source: Compiled from *The Japan Christian Year Books* (1930-1940); American Baptist Foreign Mission Society, *Annual Reports* (1930-1940); Southern Baptist Convention, *Annual of the Southern Baptist Convention* (1930-1940); Seventh-Day Adventists, *Annual Statistical Reports of the General Conference of Seventh-Day Adventists* (1930-1940).

It is obvious that parallels can be drawn at many points between the decade of the 1890's and that of the 1930's.

Thus far, we have addressed ourselves to three issues: that all churches grew during 1919-1930; that some churches were battered by adverse environment after 1930 while others apparently remained unaffected by it; and that all churches registered considerable gains through baptism though the decade of the 1930's was "most trying" to Christianity on account of the rise of the military and ultranationalism. This last fact proves that adverse environmental causes usually do not prevent growth and that the main problem lies elsewhere.

As indicated earlier, the Protestant movement in Japan after 1900 occupied itself with energetic evangelistic campaigns. This period saw similar evangelistic strategies conducted on various levels. On the cooperative side, there were the famous Kingdom of God Movement (1929-1932) and the Union Evangelistic Movement (1936-1937). Individually, all churches were engaged in frequent forward thrusts which led Iglehart to chronicle in 1931 as follows:

> There is scarcely a denomination that is not now prosecuting such a special movement throughout the church. They vary from two to five years, and as soon as one is completed its place is taken by a new one . . . most of them have linked up their own denominational program with the general one where possible.[17]

Like the early decades of this century, people flocked to these evangelistic meetings. For example, the Federal Council of Protestant Churches carried out the Kingdom of God Movement between 1929 and 1932 in conjunction with the seventieth anniversary of the Protestant mission in Japan. The central figure of this campaign was Toyohiko Kagawa. During the four years of active evangelism, the churches held 1,859 meetings, attracted an audience of 799,037, and came into contact with 62,460 who signed decision cards.[18] Naturally, not all those who signed the cards received baptism. Once again, history repeated itself; only a small segment of the audience actually fed into church membership.

One additional comment needs to be made about the church's new effort in the second phase of the Kingdom of God Movement. Kagawa was instrumental in calling the attention of the churches to the unreached masses of Japan. In the 1930's, there were approximately five million factory workers, half a million fishing folk, half a million miners, a million transport workers, and thirty million farming people.[19] The gospel was practically alien to these classes of people. Under the name of "occupational evangelism," the churches made conscientious attempts to reach them. But the results were minor. The same problems which faced the rural population plagued fishing and mining folk. "They were devoted to Buddhism and Shinto and many were even hostile to Christianity."[20] Erickson attributed the difficulty of rural evangelism to "backwardness in civilization; opposition of priests and parents and schoolteachers; hard work without clean pleasures, and the grip of the family system."[21] By the same token, the laboring class, which became more organized and expanded greatly during and after World War I, remained closed to Christianity due largely to the economic conservatism of the majority of the Protestant constituency.

> Since the Japanese Protestant churches with a constituency which was 85% middle class, were . . . conservative on economic questions, the Protestant Christian community failed both to promote social movements on labor's behalf and to develop a sizeable social program for labor at the local level.[22]

In spite of laborious efforts on the part of the church, the unreached masses of Japan stayed irresponsive to the Christian faith. So, "after two years more, in 1934 the movement quietly ended, without any public report."[23] Christianity's appeal was again limited to the white-collar class and students as before.

2. The development of the Holiness Church. The genesis of the Holiness movement in Japan is intricately related to the person of Jyuji Nakada and his encounter with the Cowmans. Without Nakada there would have been neither the Holiness Church nor its amazing growth. Therefore, we shall first sketch the life of Nakada and the growth of his movement as preparatory to our inquiry into the puzzle.

The following story is condensed from the book in Japanese, Nakada Jyuji Den.[25]

Nakada was born at Hirosaki in the prefecture of Aomori in October, 1870. When he was four, his father died leaving a wife and three sons. It is said of his childhood that he was the rowdy one of the neighborhood. One day, his concerned mother took him to a nearby Methodist church, hoping that religious teachings might change him. It was this occasion which started Nakada and his mother attending church. Though the exact facts of his baptism are not known, Yoneda concludes that Nakada was baptized in 1886 or 1887 at the age of sixteen or seventeen by a Methodist missionary named Draper. Soon he decided to become an evangelist and went to study at the Methodist-related Tokyo Eiwa Gakko (later known as Aoyama Gakuin) overcoming his financial difficulty by selling Bibles on his way to Tokyo.

At school he was an activist rather than a studious one. He devoted most of his time to practising Judo. He argued that in order to become an evangelist he had to have a strong and healthy body. Another more serious reason was that he felt the futility of theological studies. Higher criticism was just introduced to the Japanese scene. Nakada, trained in the evangelical faith, preferred the building of a sound body to surrendering his soul to what he called the "learning of death." Consequently, he was unable to graduate. With or without the degree he was determined to preach the gospel.

While serving in Oodate in Akita Prefecture, Nakada began to feel that something spiritual was lacking in him. He labored energetically in several pastorates, but soon realized that a person could not pursue his ministry too long without possessing the spiritual energy which he lacked. "Where does this spiritual energy come from?" he asked himself. Then, he recalled the scriptural passage related to the baptism of the Holy Spirit.

In his day, Dwight L. Moody was known as a great evangelist.

Nakada heard it said that Moody had received the baptism of the Holy Spirit. The figure of Moody, once an errand boy for a shoe store, who rose to influence many people appealed to Nakada who held a firm conviction that one could become an effective evangelist without much formal education. So he set sail for America in order to study at the Moody Bible Institute in December, 1896.

At the Moody Bible Institute in Chicago, Nakada attended Grace Methodist Episcopal Church. It was there that he met Mr. and Mrs. Charles Cowman. After his conversion, Mr. Cowman, a telegrapher, organized the Telegraphers Mission Band to meet regularly for the purpose of spreading the gospel. On September 3, 1894 the couple dedicated their lives for missionary service. There meeting with Nakada was just the beginning of their long, intimate friendship and comradeship in the common calling.

On November 22, 1897 there was a gathering at the Institute with an evangelist from India as a guest speaker. From the group of about fifty persons many stood up to praise God, but Nakada could not understand why he was to praise God. His heart was burdened until a thought flashed across his mind: "I don't understand why it is so, but I ought to offer praises to God for the thirst I feel for righteousness. God gave this to me." It was the turning point for him. He surrendered his all to God — his body, soul, family, and ambition to become a great preacher. His soul was calmed by inner peace as he gained the awareness of being completely sanctified.

Nakada returned to Japan in September, 1898 where he began working as a circuit preacher of the Methodist Church. As requests came in from other churches, he began to think that he ought not to be confined to one particular denomination but that he should be free to preach widely as God's evangelist. He pulled out of the Methodist church, and gradually established himself among those who, irrespective of denominational affiliations, cherished the doctrine of sanctification.

As years passed, Nakada, now an experienced evangelist, began to desire the establishment of a "city mission" where he could preach every night and operate a Bible seminary to train evangelists. It was around this time that Charles Cowman, thinking seriously of his place in God's economy, received a call to become a missionary to Japan at 10:30 p.m. on August 11, 1900. He brought the matter to his wife who unexpectedly assured him that she, too, received God's call to go to Japan six weeks before. Nakada and the couple were reunited in Japan on February 21, 1901.

The Cowmans assisted Nakada in establishing a city mission. Due to limited finance, they rented an old school building in Tokyo and called it "The Central Gospel Mission." The seminary made a humble beginning with several students.

As the work progressed, Nakada felt that they should have a name under which the Central Gospel Mission and its branch stations could be identified. With Nakada's vision that their work should eventually spread to various countries of the Orient, they decided to call themselves the Oriental Missionary Society in November, 1905.

Although the Oriental Missionary Society began as a non-denominational society, it soon took on the characteristics of a denomination and on October 31, 1917 the birth of The Japan Holiness Church was declared. The new denomination emerged with forty-six churches, fifty-seven preachers (including seven students studying at the Tokyo Bible Seminary), and about 1,600 members. Nakada was elected its first bishop.

Figure 2 graphically shows three distinct periods of Holiness growth. Until 1924 the Holiness line was parallel with those of the slow growers; it had crossed over the bottom three as early as 1915. The period that followed this relatively slow growth was astonishing. The growth line of the Holiness Church soared up through the others like a spacecraft taking off for the moon. In actual figures, the communicant membership reached 2,987 by 1924 and then climbed rapidly to 19,523 by 1932. After this year, the growth line leveled off for the next few years, and it never recovered the momentum which it had acquired in the years following 1925.

During the period after 1932 the Holiness Church faced an internal problem centering around the founder himself.[26] The doctrinal emphases had always been placed on justification, sanctification, divine healing, and the Second Coming of Christ. To this list, Nakada now wished to add a fifth point, that Christ's Second Coming would be possible only through the restoration of Israel. Therefore, he admonished the members to pray for this to take place. To many it seemed as though Nakada believed that by praying for the salvation of the Jews the Japanese as a race might be saved. This was in direct conflict with the traditional view that salvation was an individual matter.

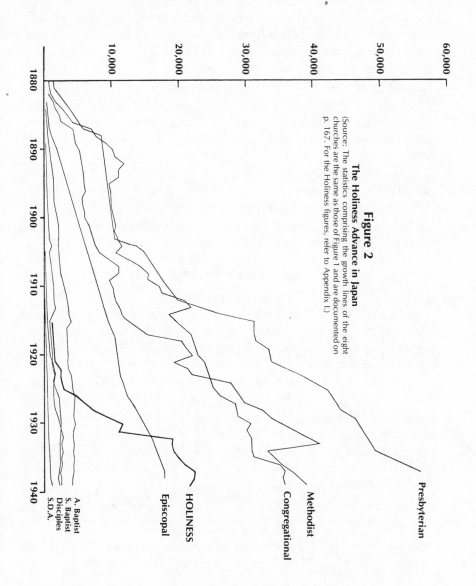

Figure 2
The Holiness Advance in Japan

(Source: The statistics comprising the growth lines of the eight churches are the same as those of Figure 1 and are documented on p. 167. For the Holiness figures, refer to Appendix I.)

Five professors of the Tokyo Bible Seminary opposed Nakada, and an emergency meeting of the Assembly was called on October 25, 1933. The Holiness Church entered into a long-drawn period of internal struggle. Even the civil court was brought in to settle the conflict but to no avail. Finally, an *ad hoc* committee on reconciliation was formed by the representatives of the Protestant church at large. Seeing the inevitability of the division, the committee attempted to bring the matter to a harmonious close. Thus, the Holiness Church was officially divided into two groups on October 19, 1936. About half of the constituency belonged to the Holiness Church (Kiyome Kyokai) headed by Nakada and the other half to the Japan Holiness Church (Nippon Sei Kyokai) led by a committee of three acting as bishops.

In our investigation of the Holiness pattern of church growth, we shall confine our analysis primarily to the period between 1924 and 1932. This pattern will in turn be contrasted with that of the eight churches. A comprehensive study of the Holiness movement is a book in itself and is obviously not attempted here.

Church Growth Interpretation

Our justification for introducing the Holiness advance lay in the hope that it might clarify the nature of growth which the eight churches had experienced during the period of this book. The following discourse is, therefore, the exposition of the two contrasting patterns of church growth.

1. The school approach pattern. Professor Sugii's data in Chapter II enabled us to define the school approach as the intellectual and individualistic response to the Christian faith. This pattern characterized the eight churches. Regardless of when they began their educational work, their converts came largely from urban middle class intellectuals and their successors who entered the church one by one. Iglehart was quite right when he wrote:

> In Japan Christianity is still largely a teaching, as is indoctrinated into individuals, slowly and thoroughly until one by one they accept it. The tradition is that no one is to be very emotional and that even if a traveling evangelist does awaken a spark of warm feeling under which decisions are made, this must be followed by months of intellectual training before one can really be said to have entered the Christian life. This may in part account for the fact that before the churches have got around to making the link-up following an evangelistic meeting, all but one or two percent of those signing cards have cooled to their former indifference, and are lost to the church.[27]

A closer examination of the school approach may help us assess the nature of its structure in the proper light. We propose to do this by introducing a study made of the ten Kyodan[28] churches in Kyoto. The underlying assumption was that the social structure of a congregation affected the spread of the Christian faith. In order to discover what the social structure was, the writer made a family analysis of ten typical Kyodan churches during the month of February, 1969.[29]

Kyodan congregations were chosen because: (1) other investigations led the writer to believe that other denominations followed the similar pattern; (2) most of the eight churches are now in the Kyodan.

Choosing typical congregations was more difficult. What was "typical" may be answered in the following way. First, it was typical in size. The Kyoto district had eighty-three churches and 6,590 communicants according to the 1969 *Kyodan Nenkan*.[30] Out of these, ten churches and 952 communicants were studied. This means that there were bigger and finer churches than the ten chosen for this study. Also, there were smaller and weaker churches than these. But, the ten chosen were the median in that they approximated the national average per church communicant membership of eighty-nine. Second, it was urban. Japanese churches have always been located in the cities. Third, it was not an institutional church. All of these churches studied were not "compound churches" on or adjacent to Christian schools. Fourth, it had a kindgergarten and a building. Nine out of ten churches ran kindergartens during the week, and all ten churches possessed a main building where worship services were held and the educational activities carried on. Fifth, it had a resident pastor living at the church. Resident pastors usually live on the church property. Sixth, it was in a typical part of the city. This meant that the ten churches were widely scattered over Kyoto. Kyoto was chosen partly because it is a typical city and partly because it was where the writer lived since he was associated with Doshisha University located in the same city. But the most important reason for choosing Kyoto was that the city, not having been bombed, had its records still intact.

The alternative ways of selecting ten churches were rejected. The writer could very easily pick out, at random, ten churches from all Kyodan churches in Kyoto. Or, he could classify Kyodan churches in Kyoto according to such categories as compound churches, very small churches, and very large churches and then choose several churches belonging to one such category. He rejected both alternatives because neither would have served his purpose of discovering the relation between the social structure and the spread of the Christian faith among the typical Kyodan churches.

The procedure of making a family analysis was as follows. In each church, the writer met with the pastor and examined the current church roll with him. On each member, he obtained the information concerning the name, sex, marital status, year of birth, year of baptism, age at the time of baptism, and family relationship among other members. He also procured some information about the occupation of the members and the status of the non-Christian members of the family. The plan was to continue the analysis until some convincing patterns emerged.

The ten churches studied are listed below with their communicant memberships.

Table 14
Communicant Memberships of Ten Kyodan Churches

Church	Founding Year	Former Denominational Affiliation	Communicants[a] In: 1967	1969
1. Muromachi	1890	Presbyterian	126	106
2. Kyoto Aoi	1907	Salvation Army	122	135
3. Kyohoku	1909	Methodist	102	78
4. Rakusai	1909	E.U.B.	73	80
5. Kyoto Omiya	1914	Presbyterian	85	87
6. Oto	1927	E.U.B.	99	134
7. Murasakino	1935	Congregational	87	73
8. Kyoto Fukko	1946	Kyodan	124	125
9. Rakunan	1946	Kyodan	96	77
10. Kinrin	1951	Kyodan	113	57

a. Communicant figures are composites of resident and non-resident members.

Source: Compiled from the 1969 *Nihon Kirisutokyodan Nenkan*, p. 336; the writer's field study of "Ten Kyodan Churches in Kyoto" conducted in Feburary, 1969.

Three churches out of ten were officially started as Kyodan churches after World War II, but each had a small congregation which began in prewar days with a denominational affiliation; Kyoto Fukko (Holiness) was begun in 1938, Rakunan (Congregational) in 1931, and Kinrin (Die Ostasien mission) in 1901.

Some difference between the 1967 and 1969 figures must be noted. There are various reasons to account for this. One natural reason is that there was a time lapse of fourteen months between two reporting periods. Also, it is highly possible that approximate numbers were reported previously in some cases. As the writer examined the names on the church roll one by one, the pastor on occasion suggested the deletion of some names for one reason or another. Several non-residents whose whereabouts were no longer known to the pastor had been unjustly kept on the roll. Such members were sorted out when the pastor and the writer reconstructed the up-to-date count of the 1969 communicant membership.

These facts gained from the family analysis have been tabulated in three tables. Table 15 and 16 (p. 124) together reveal the age distribution of 952 communicants at the time of baptism, confirmation, or induction (in the case of persons affiliated with the former Salvation Army). The prewar and postwar categories signify the persons who were baptized before 1945 and those after 1946 respectively. Figures from both tables make up the total communicant membership of each church. Further, Table 17 (p. 124) shows the distribution of total communicants according to the marital status and sex distinction. These tables are packed with lessons. However, we shall confine ourselves to the task of singling out the findings immediately relevant to the present study.

Lesson one: the age factor. In both prewar and postwar periods (see Table 15 below, and 16, p. 124), persons between the ages of twelve and twenty-two were most responsive to the Christian

Table 15
Prewar Age Distribution at the Time of Baptism Among Ten Kyodan Churches

					Church No.						
Age	1	2	3	4	5	6	7	8	9	10	Total
9-11	1	1	1	1	0	0	0	0	0	0	4
12-15	4	7	2	2	5	1	0	2	0	3	26
16-18	6	5	4	3	6	4	0	7	4	3	42
19-22	12	12	8	4	16	7	2	4	5	3	73
23-26	6	2	1	2	6	2	1	3	1	0	24
27-30	5	2	1	1	2	3	0	0	0	3	17
31-35	0	2	1	1	1	1	2	1	1	1	11
36-40	1	0	0	0	0	0	0	0	0	0	1
41-45	0	0	0	1	0	0	0	2	1	0	4
46-50	0	1	0	0	0	0	0	1	0	0	2
51-79	0	0	0	0	0	0	0	0	0	0	0
Total	35	32	18	15	36	18	5	20	12	13	204

Source: Tabulated from the writer's "Ten Kyodan Churches in Kyoto."

Table 16
Postwar Age Distribution at the Time of Baptism Among Ten Kyodan Churches

Age					Church No.						Total
	1	2	3	4	5	6	7	8	9	10	
9-11	0	1	1	1	0	0	0	0	0	0	3
12-15	0	5	4	7	1	3	4	17	2	5	48
16-18	7	27	14	16	11	32	23	19	16	10	175
19-22	27	29	18	18	7	35	18	25	16	13	217
23-26	15	12	11	7	7	19	5	6	12	5	99
27-30	3	7	4	1	6	10	3	13	4	5	56
31-35	8	8	3	6	4	7	3	7	7	1	49
36-40	4	8	0	6	2	7	3	3	4	2	35
41-45	4	3	1	2	2	3	3	3	2	1	20
46-50	1	1	3	2	2	3	3	4	0	1	20
51-79	2	2	1	4	0	2	3	9	2	1	26
Total	**71**	**103**	**60**	**65**	**51**	**116**	**68**	**105**	**65**	**44**	**748**

Source: Tabulated from the writer's "Ten Kyodan Churches in Kyoto."

Table 17
Marital Status and Sex Distribution

Church	Full Families	Half Families			Singles				Widowed		Divorced		Total		
	Couples	Members	Husbands	Wives	M -30	M 30+	F -30	F 30+	M	F	M	F	M	F	Per Church
No. 1	(21)	42	16	15	5	2	7	11	0	7	0	1	44	62	106
No. 2	(28)	56	14	30	5	1	11	6	5	7	0	0	53	82	135
No. 3	(14)	28	9	11	4	2	10	6	1	7	0	0	30	48	78
No. 4	(12)	24	10	16	7	2	8	7	0	6	0	0	31	49	80
No. 5	(21)	42	6	14	4	2	8	3	1	7	0	0	34	53	87
No. 6	(15)	30	20	49	10	2	6	6	2	7	1	1	50	84	134
No. 7	(10)	20	8	20	5	1	6	5	1	7	0	0	25	48	73
No. 8	(24)	48	9	20	14	0	14	8	0	11	1	0	48	77	125
No. 9	(11)	22	9	13	12	1	7	6	0	7	0	0	33	44	77
No. 10	(9)	18	6	8	8	3	10	0	0	3	0	1	26	31	57
Total	**(165)**	**330**	**107**	**196**	**74**	**16**	**87**	**58**	**10**	**69**	**2**	**3**	**374**	**578**	**952**

Source: Tabulated from the writer's "Ten Kyodan Churches in Kyoto."

faith. This means that sixty-one percent of all baptized were of school age. A further 12.9 percent were young people (ages 23-26) just out of school. In other words, 73.9 percent of all baptisms were received by persons between the ages of twelve and twenty-six and 81.6 percent between the ages of twelve and thirty.

From these facts, three things are made clear: (1) the prewar and postwar baptismal patterns are similar; (2) the majority of Christians in Japan was either baptized as students (or their age equivalents) or as young persons just out of school; (3) since the fourteen and fifteen year olds predominate among the persons between the ages of twelve and fifteen, it is safe to say that the lower limit of ready response was the early teens and the upper limit thirty.

Lesson two: the individual way into the church. Out of 165 couples (or 330 out of 952 communicants) shown in Table 17 (p. 124), twenty-nine were baptized in the same year. This does not indicate that all twenty-nine couples were baptized on the same day as husband and wife. Six out of twenty-nine couples are known to have received baptism before the age of sixteen years which, in the pre-war Japanese culture, is too young to be married. Most of the remaining twenty-three couples were baptized after twenty-three years of age. They were old enough to be married at the time of their baptism, though it was still too early an age for them to be economically secure. For a man, the marriageable age in Japan is much higher than twenty-three. All these facts led the writer to conclude that the most common way into the church in Japan had been the individual pattern whereby the converts joined the church one by one and not in families or groups. This pattern supports the notion that the majority of the Protestant constituency in Japan came into the church as individuals while attending schools or shortly after their graduation but before their marriage.

Lesson three: the biological growth. Examining the family relationship among the church members, the writer noted that most of 165 couples were nuclear families with no biological relationship to each other. The second and third generation Christian families were distinguished by their fewness. There were a few cases of substantial Christian lineage, but they were rare. The pastors and others whom the writer interviewed informed him that the second and third generation Christians, few as they were, usually came from the pastors' homes and the families of devout elders and deacons. This point is further verified by the fact that less than one fifth of the total number of singles (235) were the children of half and full families (where one or both parents were Christian). The dominant pattern of growth in Japan then is not biological but the growth from the world; more children of non-Christians came into the church than those of Christians. Many Christian couples were too young to have children of baptismal age. On the other hand, couples old enough to have children of high school and college age were few, and those who had some of their children in the church were still fewer. Gray haired Christians are among the minority today. There seems to be a vicious cycle of people coming in, staying a few years, and leaving. Thus, the notion of membership reduction through death must be given its proper place. The main way out of the church has been and is through membership leakage. Furthermore, the Japanese churches are largely composed of members who are the only Christians in their homes. This fact compounds the problem of membership loss.

Lesson four: the problem of half families. A significant portion, 303 out of 952 or 31.8 percent, of the total communicants constitutes half families. Although there are many examples of a Christian husband leading his wife to the faith or *vice versa*, a greater number of cases prove to be contrary. The traditional religious *milieu* of the spouse along with that of the main family and of the surrounding community often discourages the Christian wife from practicing her faith. Facing discouragement and obstruction, she tends to internalize her faith and sever her visible tie with the church, and she will eventually be lost to the church.

The other side of the problem is well described by Cressy. He writes:

> 13.2% of the membership of 54 urban churches in Japan is made up of half-Christian homes — where only one parent is a Christian. This is a major problem. From this fact it is possible and also wise to suggest that many Christians are lost to the church life because of the disinterestedness and/or opposition of the non-Christian parent.[31]

The writer's 31.8 percent may appear too high in comparison with Cressy's 13.2%. This difference will be resolved when we recall that a large constituency of students and singles in Tokyo would lower the percentages of full and half families. Tokyo has always been the mecca of education in Japan and as such gathers an unusual share of students. Massive employment opportunities in government and business await young people just out of school. Churches in Tokyo receive many such persons into their membership. Whatever the percentage of half families, Cressy's point that their offsprings are often lost to the church is a valid one.

Lesson five: the high risk of singles to the church. Approximately seventy percent of 235 singles are below the age of thirty. Marriage and the pressures of employment will absorb their time and care so that soon the church will gradually be squeezed out of their lives. These singles, upon marriage, are destined to share the problem encountered by half families.

Unmarried men above the age of thirty-one are rare in the church[32] since they are freer to find their wives, Christian or otherwise, than single women their husbands. Japanese culture considers unmarried women in their thirties marriage casualties. Many among these constitute the old faithfuls within the church. On the whole, the singles are of high risk to the church. They receive little encouragement at home. They must maneuver against the unfavorable current of traditionalism. It is not unusual for these young men and women to become victims of these obstacles.

Lesson six: the predominance of females. Of the total communicants, the ratio of men to women was two to three. This tendency has appeared since 1900, and we have already specified the high rate of falling away due to added burdens placed upon females in Japanese culture.

Our study of the social structure of the congregation reinforces what has been said of the school approach and helps underscore the structure of slow growth built on it. We shall now discuss the basic elements of this structure.

The individualistic way into the church is one such retarding element. The converts entered the church one by one completely isolated from their familial ties. The eight churches rarely experienced entrance into the church of persons in families and groups.

A second element was the way Christianity was understood as a learning. The convert joined the church after a long period of study. Many inquirers who showed interest in mass evangelistic meetings either did not subject themselves to this long course of training or lost the original zeal in the process. In either case, they were lost to the church.

A third element was its monolithic leadership structure. The task of propagation was largely left to the professional clergy. Historically, this is not difficult to understand. The laity has always been a passive recipient in Buddhist and Shinto worship services. Psychologically, the Japanese Christian could not divorce himself from the sensei-seito (master-disciple) relationship due to the heavy premium placed on learning. Sociologically, the unique character of the white-collar workers influenced the behavioral pattern in their religion. The white-collar workers including their successors internalized their faith and became less altruistic towards evangelism than their predecessors. Also, they were most keen on the principle of the division of labor. As far as they were concerned, missionaries and pastors were trained specialists on Christianity. Thus, the doctrine of the priesthood of all believers was hardly practised among them.

A fourth element was its vulnerability to membership leakage. The members who came into the church one by one through the school approach lacked moral support through web relations.

In short, our study of Kyodan churches shows that the social structure of the congregation definitely affects the spread of the gospel and that in the case of the school approach it has worked largely in the negative.

2. The conversion approach pattern. In contrast to the school approach of the eight churches, we shall deal with the conversion approach pattern of the Holiness Church. In Chapter II, the conversion approach has been defined as the experiential and group-oriented way into the church. The convert had a radical religious experience and could not contain within himself the joy of salvation. He shared the good news with his family, relatives, and friends. In this way, the essentially individualistic response to the faith often triggered group response. Sometimes, whole families and people in groups joined the church together.

In order to investigate the amazing growth of the Holiness Church, the writer conducted an interview with its leaders,[33] and portions of the interview are given verbatim below.

Question: How did the Holiness Church get started?

O: At first, Mr. Yamamori, evangelism was done every night of the year at the Central Gospel Mission in Tokyo. Many persons responded and we encouraged them to go to the nearby churches. But, these people whom we sent came back complaining that they did not fit into the churches they visited. This, I suppose, was due to the fact that these people were in the Moody tradition. That's the reason why it was decided that we should begin our own church. Thus, the Holiness Church came into being in 1917.

Y: I might add that our converts were regarded as a different brand of people by other churches. As a matter of fact, our people themselves sought a different type of worship experience.

Question: What do you consider to be the unique characteristics of the Holiness Church in prewar days?

O: When someone underwent a definite religious experience and became a member of our church, he was sure to guide other members of his family and his acquaintances to Christ. It made little difference which member of the family became converted first. Any person, who had a definite religious experience similar to those recorded in the Book of Acts, would soon lead the rest of his family to Christ. Thus, there was no majority of men or women, old or young in our congregations. For example, the Yodobashi church which I now serve has many people who are third and fourth generation Christians. Because of the web relationships that exist among the members, we experience very little membership leakage.

K: Perhaps another characteristic was the emphasis placed on salvation. We did not go about inviting people to come to church, study the Bible as seekers for a period of time, make the confession of faith, be baptized, and become a member of the church. Like Moody, we stressed the fact that if a person repented his sins and believed in Christ, he was saved then and there. That, I believe, characterized our evangelistic approach uniquely.

O: This 'instant salvation' may have offended some members of the established churches, but from our experience we can say that we produced many devout Christians with definite religious experiences.

Y: Bishop Nakada emphasized the preaching of an experiential religion.

O: After 1919, there occurred a series of revivals in the Holiness Church, and this widespread revivalism should be considered as an additional characteristic.

Question: To what geographical regions did your church spread?

O: Bishop Nakada had a vision to take the gospel to every corner of Japan.

Y: Especially to the strata of society neglected by the established churches.

O: This meant going to the most remote regions of the empire. But while doing so, the leaders realized that they were working on the irresponsive segments of Japanese society. Therefore, they soon changed their policy and worked in large and middle-sized cities.

Question: Where did the converts actually come from?

Y: Though we never aimed at evangelizing any particular class within the society, our church was successful in reaching the masses. The majority of our constituency was made up of the blue-collar workers, merchants, and their dependents.

Question: How would you describe Bishop Nakada?

O: He was a man of an unusual gift. He attracted people. The church members respected him and looked up to him as their supreme commander. In fact, whatever he said became almost a command. If he thought of something regarding the strategy of the church, his lieutenants and the laity would carry out his plan to the letter. The chain of command came down from the bishop in the form of a weekly newspaper through which the preachers and the lay members learned of the bishop's ideas. For example, Mr. Yoneda, as editor of that paper, tried to explain the bishop's new policy or idea in the paper so that the objectives might be achieved. I, as treasurer, planned the budget accordingly.

Question: What was Bishop Nakada's attitude towards educational work?

K: Bishop Nakada held that people who felt called to go into educational work should contribute to the church's cause in that field, but for people engaged in evangelism there should be no room for anything other than preaching. Therefore, we never operated educational institutions.

O: Even in running a Sunday school, the main purpose was evangelistic rather than educational.

The information contained in the above interview and in *Nakada Jyuji Den* along with other data helps us find the possible causes for the Holiness advance of 1924-1932.

First, the Holiness Church utilized the existing social structure advantageously by emphasizing the conversion of the whole family as a unit. A former Holiness member, now married to a Kyodan pastor, related to this writer that the Holiness pastor sought ways to bring in people to the church in families and groups and that the church members were encouraged to win their relatives and friends to the faith. The statements given above suggest that people in families did respond to the Christian faith. There were some obvious advantages to this approach: (1) the new converts had little danger of social dislocation leading to membership loss; (2) families of Christians would be more open (or hostile) to Christianity by their prior acquaintance with at least one Christian; (3) being joined by other members of his family, the existing church member received the spiritual and emotional support he needed to keep his faith alive and lively. The social structure of the congregation may be said to have worked in the affirmative in the case of the Holiness Church; the pitfalls related to the one-by-one pattern had been largely overcome.

Second, stress on immediate conversion was the hammer that broke the common pattern of the eight churches. The original zeal of the person who responded to the gospel was not lost due to "months of intellectual training before one can really be said to have entered the Christian life." The new convert was quickly taught the fundamentals of Christian faith and was in turn communicating the newly found faith to others.

Third, revivals deepened the spiritual life of the whole church and heightened its evangelistic zeal. The people believing in the pure gospel preached revival, expected revival, and put their faith in revival. The revival for which these people were waiting finally began to take place at Yodobashi Holiness Church in Tokyo towards the end of November, 1919. Though it spread to various churches in the city, this revival was confined to the vivification of the pastors and members. Commenting on the results of the revival of 1919-1920, Nakada listed the following four items: (1) the qualitative development of the membership; (2) an increase in giving; (3) the spiritual unity with men of other denominations (mostly pastors) who shared in the revival meetings; (4) an increase in the spirit of evangelism.[34]

On May 19, 1930 there occurred another revival,[35] this time, at the Tokyo Bible Seminary where students had been earnestly praying for revival. When suddenly the prayer meeting turned into a revival of intensity and excitement, some students recognized this to be the revival and rushed to the homes of their professors with the news. They too joined the meeting and prayed shoulder to shoulder in loud voices. There were some who even began dancing.

They continued to pray. When Nakada returned to Tokyo from his trip to Korea and Manchuria, he encouraged the Holiness churches in Tokyo to hold prayer meetings from May 30 through June 7. And on June 8, the Pentecostal meeting was held at the seminary. For the next two and a half years, various revival meetings of both large and small scale had been held in many different cities in Japan. The leaders of the Holiness Church traveled extensively, preached often, and prayed intensely.

Thus, by the end of 1930, it is reported that the Holiness Church had an accession of 4,311 reaching the total membership of 12,046. At the end of the following year, there were 3,487 conversions, 11,330 communicants, and 403 churches. One notices between these two years a considerable drop in membership, a loss of 716. I. Yoneda says that it was due to the purging of inactive members who seldom attended meetings and gave nothing to the church. The growth continued till 1932 when the membership numbered 19,523.

Fourth, the Holiness Church zealously evangelized the remote regions of the empire, but when faced with the solid wall of irresponsiveness, it shifted its emphasis to the more receptive populations in the city.

Fifth, the Holiness Church had a multiple leadership structure. Since the beginning, its denominational seminary in Tokyo existed for the purpose of training evangelists who could preach the pure gospel. The requirements to enter the seminary were minimal; the applicant should have experienced rebirth, should be able to read and write, and should be at least eighteen years old.[36] The spiritually committed persons could enter the ministry without high school or college diplomas. Further, the laity took seriously the doctrine of the priesthood of all believers. Strachan wrote: "The expansion of any movement is in direct proportion to its success in mobilizing its total membership in continuous propagation of its beliefs."[37] The Holiness Church was most successful in mobilizing its laity. The spirit filled artisan could become a leader of a churchlet (a small cell group meeting in a home), and this pattern was reproducible.

Sixth, the Holiness Church was most equipped to reach the masses and actually received its strongest support from them. In sharp contrast to the eight churches, it gathered within its membership the blue-collar workers, employers and employees of small business concerns, and their dependents. Church leadership came from among themselves. The sermons were full of interesting stories. The criterion of a good sermon was that everyone could understand what was preached from the pulpit.[38]

Seventh, Nakada through his charismatic leadership challenged the entire Holiness con tituency with high goals of attainment. On November 10, 1927 Nakada addressed the second assembly of the Holiness Church in which he stated that the success of the Holiness advance depended on its evangelism-centered policy. And the assembly ended with the proclamation that the Holiness Church would win one million souls by the time of the next assembly in 1932.[39] Nakada's word was respected and his authority commanding because what he preached worked in the convert's life and in the growth of the Holiness Church. Enthusiasm resulted from success and the amazing growth of the Holiness Church was convincing evidence of this statement.

Thus, the church generally grows when it experiences redemption and forgiveness, an infilling of God's spirit and joy in the Lord, victory over sin, going out to find "our relatives," and a religious experience so real and vivid that it could not be contained. The Holiness Church during 1924-1932 experienced all this, and it grew remarkably well. Fervent faith and burning conviction underlay the whole sociological structure. The conversion approach of the Holiness Church held the keen consciousness that the communication of the gospel and the multiplication of churches was God's will.

3. The comparison of the two contrasting patterns. In this concluding statement, we need only to point out that the Holiness Church overcame the retarding factors of the school approach pattern. It countered the intellectual and individualistic way of the eight churches with the experiential and group-oriented way. It replaced the monolithic leadership structure of the eight churches with a multiple leadership structure. By seeking the whole family as a unit, it increased the web relationships among the church members which contributed towards the lessening of membership leakage. And its emphasis on immediate conversion and subsequent indoctrination helped conserve those persons who would have been lost through the prolonged intellectual training of the eight churches.

Conclusion

The entire discourse of this book has been the response to a simple query: "Just how does the church grow in a predominantly non-Christian culture?" The answer necessitated a rather complex treatment. In this concluding section, we shall summarize the highlights of each chapter, draw some church growth insights gained from this study, and suggest the area of future research.

Chapter I (1859-1881) described the beginnings of various missions in a society which was destined to change and yet was, for the moment, heavily weighted down by the restrictions of family and hamlet. These two elements of social structure persisted throughout the period of this book strengthening the communal bonds and hampering the growth of individualism. In this connection, we have introduced Wach's thesis that a highly individualistic religion such as Christianity needed two factors that were essential for its growth: (1) a gradual emancipation of the individual from the influence of his cultural and social background; (2) a continuous process of differentiation within the civilization itself. We proposed to test our hypothesis couched in Wach's thesis: the same two factors mentioned by Wach may be essential in the development of Japanese Protestantism between 1859 and 1939.

By 1881 the Protestant movement in Japan already revealed the structure of growth which was to prevail for the rest of this study. The young people living in big cities constituted the early converts. Most of them were students. There was some response in the rural region, but even these converts were city-minded rural dwellers. With some exceptions, the common pattern of entrance into the church was one by one and the church was composed of individuals extracted from their familial contexts. From the standpoint of class orientation, the Protestant church drew its membership almost exclusively from the middle class. The descendants of the former *samurai* and the rural elite were in the majority and were actually none other than the intellectuals of the day. In a word, they were freer to respond to the gospel because they were the most detached individuals in Japanese society. And the church worked on these responsive segments of society.

The growth differentials among the five churches were also evident. The Presbyterian, Congregational, and Methodist Churches respectively registered a considerable number of converts in this exploratory period. They were more successful than the Episcopal and American Baptist Churches in making contacts with the people responsive to the gospel because these three had more missionaries and nationals who were better equipped for the task.

Chapter II (1882-1889) described the factors which created Japan's openness to the West and analyzed the structure of growth. In the 1880's, Japan became extremely hospitable to Western ideologies because of the revolution of the seventies, the progress on the agrarian-industrial spectrum, the relative freedom from fear of foreign domination, and the pressure for treaty revision. Those who responded to Western influence, however, were limited to a particular portion of the population. They were the urban upper-and-middle class intellectuals and their protégés. Thomas, Sugii, and others testified that the Protestant church in Japan gathered its membership from among those who demonstrated affinity towards the West. Thus, we confirmed our notion that the sector of society which was most open to the West was at the same time most responsive to the Christian faith.

Once again, the largest number of converts in this period came from among the students, notably in mission schools. They were often the only Christians in their homes.

Congregational and Presbyterian Churches grew fastest and did so because they had the greatest number of missionaries; trained the national forces quickly; organized more churches with many of them self-supporting; concentrated their churchly forces in strategic places; emphasized education, self-support, and simplicity of worship; and attracted many able nationals to their memberships with their representative form of government.

Chapter III (1890-1902) witnessed the effects upon the churches of Japan's waning enthusiasm towards the West. The facts of growth informed us that not all the churches were equally affected by it. In fact, it was a difficult period for Congregational and Presbyterian churches but others found it rather favorable. We gave the following four reasons for this phenomenon: (1) These two churches had the highest rate of membership leakage. (2) Their mission schools experienced marked decrease in student enrollments. (3) They had a large share of "fair-weather Christians" in government circles and among the upper class whom they lost with the shift in climate. (4) Their evangelistic zeal and efforts were heavily curtailed by two factors: the "clamor for independence" in national affairs which was echoed in matters ecclesiastical and skepticism which accompanied radical views from the West to take the fire out of the evangelistic enterprises. The Congregational and Presbyterian Churches suffered more than any other church from the independence movement and liberal theology. Perhaps, this fourth factor was the blow that took the heartbeat of heretofore rapidly growing churches.

Insofar as environment influences church growth, we have concluded that there are three major ways in which adverse environmental factors can operate. First, they make it more difficult to become Christian but usually they do not prevent conversion. Second, decrease of the conversion rate reduces the efficiency of the mission machine by chilling the church's evangelistic fervor, drastically diminishing evangelistic forces, and freezing their activities. Third, they work against church growth by fostering membership leakage.

Chapter IV (1903-1918) sought to answer three key questions concerning Japanese church growth for the early decades of this century. First, why did the phenomenon of Christian resurgence take place? We replied by saying that the Protestant movement in general poured out its aggressive evangelistic effort on the most receptive segment of society. Due to industrialization, there emerged a group of white-collar workers and this group grew as time passed.

Second, why did the church grow almost exclusively among the white-collar class? The white-collar workers were most mobile and free of old traditions and social relations. They were open to new ideas from the West and Christianity appealed to some of them. In the process of seeking greater power and higher status, they often experienced *anomie* and some of them found an answer in the church. The general atmosphere of the Protestant church was one of extreme intellectualism. Even in mass rallies, the speakers were members of the intellectual elite such as noted pastors and Christian scholars and therefore only the white-collar people and their protégés responded. And again, the people of this class were relatively free to pursue time-consuming church activities. Further, we may point out that the growth of individual consciousness was limited to this class and people belonging to this class experienced the frustration of the ego more than anyone else in Japanese society. The Christian faith for various reasons was judged tenable by this class.

Third, what contributed to the widening of the gulf between expansionists and slow growers? We have given several reasons, but we may summarize them by saying that the expansionists possessed better mission machines, planned definite, comprehensive strategies of evangelism, and developed a strong sense of "our mission" in carrying on the evangelistic work.

Chapter V (1919-1939) attempted to contrast two distinct patterns of church growth. We have learned that the school approach pattern contained within it the structure of slow growth in contrast to the conversion approach pattern of the Holiness Church. Some of the elements of this slow growth structure were: (1) the individualistic way into the church, (2) the way of looking at Christianity as a learning, (3) the monolithic leadership structure, (4) the vulnerability to membershp leakage. On the other hand, we have stated that the Holiness Church countered these retarding elements through various emphases. Further insights from the comparison of these patterns will be mentioned in our discussion of the structure of rapid growth.

Now we wish to make some conceptual observations about church growth in prewar Japan.

As we have stated, Japanese Protestantism developed along definite class lines. In the case of the eight churches, the majority of the members was constituted by urban middle class intellectuals and their successors throughout the whole period. Though the components of the middle class before and after 1900 differed somewhat, they were nevertheless the people in each period who were most detached from the traditional *milieu*. Even with an emphasis placed on occupational evangelism after 1930, the respondents to Christianity were narrowly confined to the same class. The eight churches were unable to reach the farming, laboring, and fishing classes whose life style was quite communal. On the other hand, the Holiness Church did receive a marked response from the laboring masses in urban areas. The Holiness Church was thus successful in bringing into the church some people whom the eight churches failed to reach. Despite its conscientious effort to win the people neglected by the established churches, the Holiness Church could not, however, reach the people in the rural region. This simply means that the Protestant church in Japan, regardless of its patterns, was an urban movement.

Second, our hypothesis couched in Wach's thesis is generally plausible but not universally applicable. It is plausible in the case of the eight churches which grew primarily among the people in Japanese society who were most emancipated from their cultural and social background. Most of them lived in the region where cultural diffusion was rapidly taking place. On the other hand, our hypothesis does not apply completely in the case of the Holiness Church. While it too was confined to the urban region, its primary success was among the masses whose life style was heavily communal and among whom the birth of individuation was slow to develop. The family ideology was very strong. How are we to account for this phenomenon? Certainly, the Holiness advance did not depend on the emancipation of the individual. Freedom from one's cultural and social background was not "essential" in the sense that growth depended on it.

Finally we may seek clues to rapid growth. Such growth occurs when the church: (1) utilizes the prevailing social structure to its advantage; (2) overcomes the notion of Christianity as a learning by the program of immediate conversion followed by careful Christian nurture; (3) possesses fervent faith in the saving God and an impassioned zeal for evangelism; (4) concentrates on the responsive population which it is uniquely equipped to reach; (5) develops a multiple leadership structure which mobilizes its entire lay membership; (6) acknowledges the various homogeneous units within the society and creates a multi-dimensional leadership structure which best suits the various social units; (7) follows a definite, comprehensive strategy of evangelism with a high goal of reaching many persons; and (8) devises a way to prevent membership leakage by a conscientious attempt to build Christian families.

In the following, we shall suggest areas of further research which could reveal a more complete picture of the structure of church growth in Japan.

First, research may be conducted to investigate in more detail the conversion approach pattern by contrasting the pattern of the Holiness Church with that of the former Nagasaki or Kirishitan communities, with that of the Spirit of Jesus Church soon after World War II, and with that of the Soka Gakkai after 1950.

Second, studies should be made of the cases with notable growth in the postwar period to see if their patterns might differ from the ones described in this book.

In dealing with this rather vast topic, the writer conscientiously attempted to fill a gap in the systematic study of church growth in prewar Japan. Others will surely correct what is not right in this book, but the writer takes comfort in the belief that this piece of work will serve as a springboard for further dialogue and discussion on the topic of church growth in Japan.

The Soka Gakkai:
A Religious Phoenix

Reprinted from PRACTICAL ANTHROPOLOGY
Volume 19, Number 4 (July-August 1972)

The phenomenal growth of Soka Gakkai in postwar Japan is analyzed in terms of creed, cult, code, and organization. The creed is simple, utilitarian, tradition-oriented, eschatological, and nationalistic. Cult increases the sense of belonging and personal worth and emphasizes making converts. The this-worldly, egalitarian moral code gives even persons from the lowest classes a sense of worth. A complex interlocking network of vertical, horizontal, and diagonal groupings permits maximum participation and minimizes leakage. The Christian church should learn from this sect to reach all groups in society, to emphasize Christian joy, to foster every-member witnessing, to mobilize the laity and develop multiple leadership, and to encourage whole-family conversion.

From the ashes of the Second World War in Japan arose a powerful and fast growing religious movement which claimed its heritage in the thirteenth century Buddhist reformer Nichiren. It is called the Soka Gakkai, literally translated into English as the Value-Creating Society. The metamorphosis of the Soka Gakkai can be likened to the rise of a phoenix and its growth fittingly described by no other adjective than the word "phenomenal".

To be sure, much success in gaining converts on the part of the so-called new religions has been a commonplace in postwar Japan. What is not common, however, is the phenomenon of that rapid, sky-rocketing growth which only the Soka Gakkai has been able to achieve in so short a time. The following table reveals the growth of the Soka Gakkai during the last two decades in comparison with the progress made by some prominent new religions.[1]

Group	1950	1955	1960	1964	1968[2]
Soka Gakkai	9,000	900,000	5,000,000	14,000,000	19,854,000
Rissho Koseikai	312,305	1,122,973	1,618,733	1,980,348	
PL Kyodan	276,075	543,604	983,394	1,164,814	
Seicho-no Ie	956,420	1,469,844	1,530,108	1,477,140	
Sekai Kyuseikyo	164,785	385,644	415,428	591,133	

The table shows that the Soka Gakkai began its growth rather late compared with others, but the rate of its growth surpasses all of them. Also it becomes evident that the Soka Gakkai has continued its fast growth during the last two decades, while others have either levelled off or maintained minimal growth. How has the Soka Gakkai been able to achieve such a growth? Though there have appeared numerous popular and scholarly articles and a few books dealing with Japan's new religions in general and the Soka Gakkai in particular, works investigating its phenomenal growth are few. This article concerns itself primarily with the analysis of the possible causes which made for its growth and should be of interest to students of church growth.

The Creedal Aspect

No single theory of growth, whether of hope, aggressive evangelistic fervor, group dynamics, or organizational efficiency, adequately explains the Soka Gakkai's unusual expansion. To get at the true causes, we must utilize a more comprehensive approach. The causes given below are analyzed in terms of creed, cult, code, and organization. Many of the causes discussed here in connection with the Soka Gakkai's growth may also apply to the success of other new religions in varying degrees, but all of them put together explain why and how only the Soka Gakkai has been able to outstrip other modern religious movements in such a unique way as to fill the spiritual void of postwar Japan, especially among the masses, in harmony with the Japanese ethos.

We begin with the creedal aspect of the Soka Gakkai's growth. Inasmuch as Tsunesaburo Makiguchi's theory of value is the bedrock of the Soka Gakkai's teaching, it is well to review it. Endo summarizes it as follows:[3]

1. The end of human life lies in the pursuit of happiness.

2. The content of happiness is not the pursuit of truth, but the creation of value.

3. There are both positive and negative values.

4. Positive value consists of beauty, profit and good; negative value consists in ugliness, harm and evil.

5. The end of human life is to win positive value in terms of beauty, profit and good.

6. Now, beauty is temporal value, profit is individual value, and good is social value.

7. Unless man seeks good, he cannot be really happy.

8. In good, there is major good, medium good and minor good. The end of human life is to realize major good, and this can only be done by believing in the only religion: The *Nichiren Shoshu*. Furthermore, the life of major good guarantees to an individual both beauty and profit.

Here we see the union of Makiguchi's value theory with the religion of the Nichiren Shoshu (the orthodox branch of the Nichiren Sect), but the connection between the two is made rather artificially. It was Josei Toda, Makiguchi's successor, who made the teachings of the Soka Gakkai appealing to the masses by subjecting the theory of value to the doctrines of the Nichiren Shoshu.

The basic faith of this sect informs the member of the Soka Gakkai that faith in the Worship Object (the *Mandala* or the *Gohonzon)* is sufficient for him to enter the state of buddhahood in his present existence. The *satori* (enlightenment) can be obtained by simply gazing at the Mandala and repeating the Daimoku in front of it. According to *Doctrines of Nichiren Shoshu,*

> the supreme law of Buddha is perceived by everyone in the Gohon-
> zon. People today, although they are not at all equal to Sakyamuni in
> their penetration of mind or observation of rules, will be able to attain
> enlightenment, get rid of delusion, and contribute towards the estab-
> lishment of lasting world peace—all just by earnest chanting of the
> fundamental prayer, the Daimoku, before the Gohonzon.[4]

Thus, faith in the Worship Object symbolizes the believer's faith in Nichiren (the true Buddha in the period of the Latter Law, 1050 A.D. to present), in the sacred scriptures (the Lotus Sutra), and in the availability of the salvation promised to the worshipper.[5] The

Daimoku refers to the prayer, "Namu myo-ho renge-kyo" (Hail to the Wonderful Law of the Lotus Sutra). It is said that the more one repeats this prayer the more merit is piled up toward his happiness in this world and the world to come.

What are some of the factors affecting the growth of the Soka Gakkai that are related to the creedal aspect?

1. The Soka Gakkai's teaching is simple. To the fundamental human quest "What must I do to be saved?" the Soka Gakkai replies: "Believe only in the Worship Object and recite the Daimoku, and you will be saved." Belief in the concrete object and belief in the magical incantation of the Daimoku, stripped of ontological and metaphysical discourses, are conducive to the Japanese religious ethos.

2. The Soka Gakkai's teaching is utilitarian. The notion of "happiness" dominates its message. "The end of human life lies in the pursuit of happiness." Happiness refers to basic material satisfaction such as economic prosperity, freedom from personal habits and adversity, long life, sound health, and domestic harmony. Toda even interpreted the state of buddhahood to possess "a cheerful happy home, a secure, vigorous spirit, a business and home life bubbling over with joy."[6] The attainment of happiness (and of buddhahood) is related to the only, true religion of the Soka Gakkai. Everyone yearns for prosperity and peace of mind. Especially, if a person is deprived of such blessings, he is quick to respond to such appeals. The emphasis on the material blessing goes well with the materialism of postwar Japan.

3. The Soka Gakkai's teaching is tradition-oriented. In a country which continues to regard Christianity as a "foreign religion" despite its long history on its soil, any religion to become popular must have a proper place in the tradition. The Soka Gakkai traces its religious heritage back to Nichiren who exerted his influence as a religious leader in the thirteenth century.

4. The Soka Gakkai's teaching is eschatological in hope. The hope of the better world is ever appealing to the disinherited.[7] In this sense, Werner Kohler, in his *Die Lotus-Lehre: Und Die Modernen Religionen in Japan*[8] (The Lotus Doctrine and the Modern Religions in Japan), considers hope to be the single most important factor in explaining the growth of the new religions in Japan. Kohler is right in his emphasis on hope, but it must be said that hope is only one of the many factors affecting the Soka Gakkai's notable growth.

Happiness, the Soka Gakkai claims, can be attained in this world. And furthermore, *any* person is capable of achieving it *now*. This is the message of the Soka Gakkai. The hope for a better day has been a source of moral encouragement to the disinherited to cope with the brutal reality of contingency, powerlessness, and scarcity in postwar Japan.

5. The Soka Gakkai's teaching is both nationalistic and internationalistic. The Nichiren Shoshu (consequently, the Soka Gakkai) reveres Nichiren as the Buddha for the present age. He, very conveniently, was a Japanese. Although the Soka Gakkai aspires to be internationalistic with the motto of *chikyu minzokushugi* (universal brotherhood), it is quite conscious of its Japanese origin. The Soka Gakkai skillfully utilizes

> traditional Japanese symbols such as the Rising Sun, the Japanese fan, and Mount Fuji, and its songs consistently emphasize such notions as that "with Japan as the base, we will throw a bridge to every nation on the earth."[9]

The true source of comfort in the nationalistically based internationalism of the Soka Gakkai lay in its message that one defeated people could actually be the chosen people to realize the global salvation. In the early 1950's, around the time of the Peace Treaty (September 8, 1951), the wounded national consciousness was gradually recovering from its "occupation mentality," to coin a phrase expressing the psychological damage inflicted upon the Japanese mind by the loss of face which resulted from the defeat in the Pacific War. Many Japanese were able to recover their illfated mentality by identifying themselves with the country's rapid economic prosperity. But there were many in the segment of society who were bypassed by it. To them, the Soka Gakkai's appeal to the latent feelings of national superiority was a much needed means of compensation. It was around this time that Toda was elected the president of the Soka Gakkai and the movement was well on its way toward great accession.

The Cultic Aspect

The worship of the Soka Gakkai member takes place on different levels. At home, he sits before the family altar in which a Gohonzon (a miniature of the one inscribed by Nichiren) is carefully stored and recites the Lotus Sutra prayer five times (*goza*) in the morning and three times *(sanza)* in the evening. He also recites the ritualistic prayer (the Daimoku) as often as possible.

In the group meetings of an intimate sort (which are usually conducted in the homes of the members and rarely in the temples of the Nichiren Shoshu), the members are encouraged to share their personal experiences after the fashion of revival meetings. Without fear of rejection, the member can unload a burdened heart about a drunken husband, nagging mother-in-law, or financial difficulty. Anything under the sun is discussed in this group meeting guided by a group leader.[10] Here the members give testimonies regarding the "divine favors" *(goriyaku)* gained through their faith in and obedience to the Soka Gakkai's way of life.

At Taiseki-ji, the main temple of the Nichiren Shoshu, the Soka Gakkai pilgrims participate in the worship service known as the *ushitora*. This service has been in existence for 670 years. Several thousand members are ushered into the large worship hall at midnight. For about twenty minutes they continuously recite the Daimoku. The amplified voices of several thousand people create a unique, hypnotic effect upon the crowd. Then, the chief priest of the temple reads part of the Lotus Sutra. Then, once again, the voices chant the Daimoku accompanied by ear-splitting beats on the drums. At 1:30 a.m., the crowd is led back to their sleeping quarters.

Through the worship of these varied types, the Soka Gakkai members increase their sense of belonging to both the "beyond" and the peer-group. The effervescent spirit in the group meeting fills the individual members with zeal. The zeal is expressed in their *shakubuku* activity, for the Soka Gakkai tells them that faith that is not expressed in *shakubuku* is insufficient. Happiness is attainable only through the accumulation of merits by winning converts. *Shakubuku*, then, signifies the break-and-subdue method of persuading converts. Worship on all levels helps the members heighten their sense of vocation—the vocation which is none other than the winning of new converts. Thus, the cultic aspect of the Soka Gakkai is directly related to the creation of aggressive evangelistic fervor among the members and consequently to its phenomenal growth.

The Aspect of Moral Code

No rigid moral code binds the Soka Gakkai members. If a person were engaged in excesses of any this-worldly pleasure, be it drinking, gambling, or sex, he cannot be happy. He is therefore admonished to follow a common-sense, "golden mean" type of morality.[11] A well-adjusted life is what everyone wants and it is what the Soka Gakkai requires of its members. This is not difficult to follow. It is quite in harmony with the ethic of Japanese society.

Another factor within the aspect of moral code relates to the Soka Gakkai's egalitarian ethic. The Soka Gakkai claims the equality of all members at the time of their entry. Neither one's age, nor his sex, nor his social position matters. The male and the female, the young and the old, the rich and the poor are all put on equal footing. On the basis of his individual effort and capability, the convert advances toward a higher rank, from an ordinary member to the rank of "Professor" through variously graded titles. According to his rank, he is put in charge of responsibilities of various degrees of importance. The function of this ranking system is quite contrary to the reality of Japanese society where differences in sex, age, and social position greatly influence his road to success. In the Soka Gakkai, the function of ranks is thought of as being socio-psychological in that the system gives status to those whom the world has overlooked. It means that the system is value-creating for the individual member.[12]

The Soka Gakkai's this-worldly, egalitarian ethic no doubt appeals to the disinherited within Japanese society and is definitely an additional factor explaining the growth achieved by the Soka Gakkai.

The Organizational Aspect

The Soka Gakkai is a lay movement of the Nichiren Shoshu. It has no priest. Only the president and some two hundred people working in the publications department are on the payroll.

The organizational structure is cellular in nature. The social relations of the laity are promoted through the vertical, horizontal, and diagonal groupings of the members.

The vertical grouping is based on conversion ties. The grouping extends from the individual, to the *kumi* (squad with 10 to 15 members), to the *han* (company with 30 to 100 members), to the *chiku* (district with 500 to 1000 members), the *shibu* (region), the *soshibu* (general region), the *chiho hombu* (local headquarters), and the *hombu* (central headquarters, located in Tokyo).[13] This can be compared with the kinship ties which are so important in Japanese culture. Member A, converted by Member B, belongs to the *kumi* of the latter person even after the former gets his own *kumi*. A *han*, therefore, is made up of those who are converted by the same group of people.

The horizontal grouping is based on geography. Japan's mobility rate is growing larger and larger. The geographically-based structure called the "block system" has been devised in order to combat the membership loss by mobility. The members in the same geographical unit keep close contact with each other, which is in itself an attack on the *anomie* created in today's rapidly changing society.

The final grouping (diagonal) is based on age, sex, and/or interest. There are various groups and activities in this category: one group each for young men, young women, college students, and housewives, athletic groups; a culture organization called *Min'on* for music, drama, dance, and cultural activities; and a political party called the Komeito.[14]

What contributions does the organizational structure of the Soka Gakkai make toward its growth?

1. Low membership requirements. The Soka Gakkai is "cheap". There are no membership dues. Once a person becomes converted, he is taken to the nearest Nichiren Shoshu temple for a twenty-five-minute ritual ceremony. Each new member receives a Gohonzon to which he is required to recite the Lotus Sutra prayer five times in the morning and three times in the evening. He promises that he will lead at least three persons to the Soka Gakkai faith. And if he subscribes to the organization's newspaper, that is about all he must do in order to participate in the various activities sponsored by the Soka Gakkai.

2. The incentive system. Earlier in connection with the egalitarian ethic, we mentioned the way in which even the persons at the low socioeconomic level can receive status denied them by the outside world. Here we need only to reiterate the points stressing its motivational aspect. Any member can attain the status of an instructor or professor by winning a certain number of converts. A mere doorman at a department store can rise to the rank "instructor" and be put in charge of a sizeable group as a leader. Such a merit system creates incentive to work harder at the task of persuading others to the faith.

3. An answer to *anomie*. In a highly industrialized, urban culture

it is inevitable that there shall be many anomic individuals. Japan's many cities are more and more falling in line with the big cities of the world. Such anomic persons are found among those who have just moved from a tightly-knit rural community to a big city, among middle-aged housewives with no children to worry about but neglected by their husbands, among students of the "wrong" (second-rate) universities, among persons in marginal occupations, among those who, while intelligent, have limited formal education, and among such like persons.[15] The Soka Gakkai's face-to-face contact approach allows its members to overcome *anomie* and yet its cellular structure permits the organization to grow into gigantic size.

4. The best use of societal *milieu*. The Soka Gakkai is sensitive to the shift of value-orientations in postwar Japan. It has been quite adroit in blending two types of involvement: the mass (collectivity-orientations) and the personal (self-orientations), the vertical and the horizontal, the hierarchical and the democratic, the central power structure and the small local groups. Lee expresses well what is meant here:

> At a time in Japanese society when the pendulum has swung from an excessive emphasis on order to a freedom that frequently borders on sheer chaos, the proper balance between freedom and order—between liberty and licence—is a much desired relief.[16]

The Soka Gakkai is well equipped organizationally to fill the spiritual void or the societal deficiency of postwar Japan.

5. The charismatic leadership. The original founder of the Soka Gakkai was a theoretician and educator under whose leadership the movement did not quite get under way. The second leader, Toda, was endowed with the gift of organizational skill and helped the Soka Gakkai grow fast. But it seems that the designation of a charismatic leader can be more appropriately given to the third and current president, Daisaku Ikeda. He is young and is said to be handsome, dynamic, and an even more talented and competent organizer than Toda.[17] He possesses a magnetic personality. He readily fills the spiritual vacuum of the masses in their latent need for an authoritarian figure. One might go so far as to suggest, at this point, that for many within the membership Ikeda would become an emperor surrogate. The role of the charismatic leader has a definite place in the growth of any successful movement. Such appears also to be the case with the Soka Gakkai.

6. A built-in mechanism against membership leakage. A mass movement is often plagued by a high attrition rate. The Soka Gakkai, however, seems to overcome this malady by creating a tight-knit web of relationships through the vertical, horizontal, and diagonal groupings. It is reported that "the Soka Gakkai . . . strongly stresses total family conversion."[18]The measure of reaching the whole family as a unit further strengthens the web relations and helps keep the attrition rate at minimum. Since the evangelistic zeal of the member is kept high by the emphasis placed on winning converts, one more danger in membership loss seems to be eliminated.

Summary of Growth Factors

It may be concluded that the Soka Gakkai has grown because (1) it has a unique message that appeals especially to the disinherited in postwar Japan; (2) the experience of worship in a small or mass meeting is directly related to the creation of aggressive evangelistic fervor which issues in *shakubuku* activities; (3) its this-worldly, egalitarian ethic is in harmony with the Japanese ethos and meets the socio-psychological needs of the segment of society from which the majority of the Soka Gakkai members have come; and (4) its organizational structure facilitates a high degree of socialization among the members to overcome *anomie,* prevents membership leakage often caused by geographical mobility, helps achieve the maximum mobilization of its entire membership for evangelism through its incentive system and emphasis on winning converts, and buttresses web relations by stressing total family conversion so as to eliminate social dislocation. This last item is especially important. Any movement largely made up of members extracted from their families is destined to slow growth due to social dislocation and ostracism in the family. The Soka Gakkai has utilized its structural mechanism to fit within the Japanese social structure and abide by its communal principle which still dominates social relationships.

Implications for Church Growth

What implications does the Soka Gakkai's rapid expansion have to church growth in Japan?

First, the Christian church in Japan must explore effective means of communicating the gospel to each of the various homogeneous units within the society. The Protestant constituency has always been made up predominantly of urban middle-class intellectuals. The Soka Gakkai's success among the masses teaches us that there is a dire spiritual need which the church in Japan has been unable to meet. The sermons preached from the pulpits are often extremely intellectual and theologically sophisticated but have not attracted the masses. The Word must be proclaimed in such a way that it becomes incarnate in the soul of every listener, whether he is from a city or a village, rich or poor, educated or uneducated. The theme of happiness obtainable during this lifetime dominates the message of the Soka Gakkai and seems to fill the spiritual and psychological void of the masses. Is it not possible for the Christian to talk about the joy and happiness in this life and for the church to translate Christian optimism into the flesh and blood of the daily life of the common people without making false promises?

Second, the experience of worship must be such that it strengthens the fiber of the believer's conviction in the redeeming God and generates unflagging zeal and energy for witnessing. In the Soka Gakkai, worship is directly related to *shakubuku* activities. Winning new converts is expected of every worshipper. In Christianity, worship is the source of vital living and the experience of worship must always be so real and so vivid to the worshipper that he cannot contain within himself the feeling of joy and happiness until they find their expression in sharing with others the joyous life found in Christ. The understanding of Christianity as a matter only of the head and not of the heart has often made Japanese Christians timid in their witnessing activities.

Third, Protestantism in Japan must mobilize the laity for evangelism. The key to the Soka Gakkai's success is due largely to its ability to mobilize the entire membership for the propagation of its faith. The doctrine of the "priesthood of all believers" must be taken more seriously and put into practice. Every Christian is under God's mandate to *minister* to others—Christian *as well as* non-Christians — for their spiritual well-being.

Fourth, the church must devise a multiple leadership structure. The Soka Gakkai created the variously graded positions of leadership for the more able members. These leaders are unpaid and therefore the structure is readily reproducible. Since they come from the group, they know their people and others like them intimately and are more capable of communicating to them. In the Japanese church, the topic of lay leadership has often been discussed but largely remained an item of theological interest. Consequently, the monolithic structure with the pastor as the sole leader has prevailed and is the most common pattern today. Is it not conceivable to develop, for example, an army of unpaid part-time lay evangelists—with proper status given them—whose task is to evangelize the unevangelized? These men and women may be assigned to full-time pastors of various churches. Not all the pastors and evangelists need to be full-time and B.D. or M.Div. graduates. Earlier, we emphasized the importance of acknowledging the various homogeneous units within the society before an effective communication of the gospel could take place. Perhaps, it is equally important to acknowledge the possible damage caused by the distance that lies between the levels of education attained by the minister and his parishioners. The various segments of society demand different types of ministers with varying degrees of experience and education. The church must consider seriously the establishment of levels of ministry—paid and unpaid, full and part-time — with due status given to all.

Fifth, the perennial problem of church growth in Japan has been membership leakage. The church has never lacked converts though there were fewer of them at "hard times." The virtual standstill or decline in membership was brought about by the members leaving the church after a few years of church life due to transfer or falling away. There appears to be a cycle of converts coming into the church, staying for a while, and leaving.

The Soka Gakkai combats this problem by (1) emphasizing the conversion of the whole family as a unit so as to avoid social dislocation and ostracism; (2) structuring an efficient organizational network based on conversion ties, geography, age, sex, and interest which enables a high degree of socialization among the members to meet the needs of the anomic persons and to galvanize the web of relations; (3) avoiding the spiritual freeze of the converts by constantly recharging their enthusiasm through experiences of worship and *shakubuku* activities.

The pattern of entrance into the church in Japan has been one by one. This means that the converts, mostly young and before marriage, join the church extracted from their familial contexts. Normal Christian living gets disrupted under such circumstances. Thus, many of them after a few years of church life fall away mainly from the hardship caused by their isolated and lonely existence. The church's conscious attempt to reach the whole family may reduce this hardship. The Soka Gakkai benefited from its family emphasis and so did the Japan Holiness Church in prewar days.

The idea of a "house church" may be tried with a lay leader or an unpaid evangelist in charge. There have been some worthy experiments. After the fashion of the Soka Gakkai, such a house meeting advances the socialization of the members in a dynamic group relationship, reduces the number of "spiritual dropouts," and is readily reproducible. Further, the loss by geographical mobility may be lessened by a closer working relationship among the churches within a denomination or by ecumenical cooperation through an operative referral system. Whatever else the church may do, it must solve the problem of membership loss by examining its current program and organizational structure. Membership leakage is a major deterrent to church growth in Japan.

Appendix A

Communicant Membership of the Presbyterian Church

Year	Communicants	Year	Communicants
1872	12	1913	23,063
1877	623	1914	26,166
1881	1,642a	1915	31,561
1885	4,807	1917	31,589
1887	6,084	1918	31,938
1888	8,690	1919	33,668
1903	10,893	1921	34,044
1904	13,830	1923	38,344
1905	15,076	1925	42,300
1907	16,287	1928	44,762
1908	17,017	1929	46,438
1910	18,460	1934	49,717
1912	20,573	1937	56,325

a. Taken from James A. Cogswell, "A History of the Work of the Japan Mission of the Presbyterian Church in the United States, 1885-1960" (Unpublished Th.D. dissertation, Union Theological Seminary, Richmond, Virginia, 1961), p. 22.

Source: James A. Cogswell, Letter to the writer (February 9, 1962).

Appendix B

Communicant Membership of the Methodist Church

Year	North (1873)a	South (1886)b	Canadian (1873)c	Total
1882	574		272	846
1883	907		377	1,284
1884	1,296		465	1,761
1885	1,754		591	2,345
1886	1,970		781	2,751
1887	2,854	71	1,283	4,208
1888	2,961	163	1,538	4,662
1889	2,815	232	1,686	4,733
1890	3,061	318	1,819	5,198
1891	3,118	381	1,928	5,427
1892	3,205	505	1,987	5,697
1893	3,335	507	1,981	5,823
1894	3,378	552	2,070	6,000
1895	3,369	547	2,137	6,053
1896	3,524	542	2,268	6,334
1897	2,966	559	2,370	5,895
1898	3,023	600	2,322	5,945
1899	3,153	666	2,374	6,193
1900	3,199	688	2,355	6,242
1901	3,516	744	2,636	6,896
1902	3,460	855	2,750	7,065
1903	3,369	1,000	2,975	7,344
1904	3,600	1,212	2,895	7,707
1905	3,653	1,417	3,105	8,175
1906		1,573	3,318	

a. The North figures are taken from Methodist Episcopal Church, Missionary Society, *Annual Reports of the Missionary Society of the Methodist Episcopal Church,* 1884-1906. The 1882 figure, however, is from Dorothy Woodruff, Letter to the writer (March 29, 1962).

b. The South figures are taken from Methodist Episcopal Church, South, Board of Missions, *Annual Reports of the Board of Missions,* 1888-1906 (Nashville, Tenn.: Publishing House of the Methodist Episcopal Church, South).

c. The Canadian figures are taken from Methodist Church (Canada), *Annual Reports of the Missionary Society of the Methodist Church,* 1883-1906 (Toronto: Methodist Mission Rooms).

Year	Communicants	Year	Communicants
1907	11,161	1922	21,309
1908	11,153	1923	22,516
1909	9,948	1924	27,934
1910	10,270	1925	28,789
1911	10,558	1927	30,088
1912	10,858	1928	32,783
1913	11,295	1929	33,819
1914	11,917	1930	35,696
1915	12,750	1933	41,682
1916	14,089	1934	33,180
1917	15,466	1935	34,453
1918	20,745	1936	35,932
1919	21,233	1937	37,188
1920	22,130	1939	39,381
1921	19,276		

Source: Dorothy Woodruff, then Research Librarian of Board of Missions of The Methodist Church, Letter to the writer (March 20, 1962). In 1907, the three branches of the Methodist Church merged to form The Japan Methodist Church (Nippon Mesodesuto Kyokai).

Appendix C

Communicant Membership of the Congregational Church

Year	Communicants	Year	Communicants
1880	722	1908	15,786
1881	881	1909	15,384
1882	1,097	1910	17,427
1883	1,877	1911	17,816
1884	2,856	1912	21,170
1885	3,569	1913	22,194
1886	4,226	1914	18,745
1887	7,093	1915	19,493
1888	7,871	1916	21,160
1889	9,146	1917	22,068
1890	10,142	1920	23,084
1891	10,760	1921	24,044
1892	12,081	1922	24,237
1893	11,079	1925	25,491
1894	11,162	1926	26,483
1895	9,863	1927	27,839
1896	10,025	1929	29,116
1897	10,081	1930	31,167
1898	10,016	1931	30,497
1899	10,214	1932	31,401
1900	10,545	1934	31,147
1901	10,856	1935	31,754
1902	10,693	1936	35,380
1904	11,908	1937	36,237
1905	10,989	1938	35,959
1906	12,604	1939	36,179
1907	14,639		

Source: American Board of Commissioners for Foreign Missions, *Annual Report, American Board of Commissioners for Foreign Missions,* 1881-1903, 1905-1918, 1920-1923, 1926-1928, 1930-1933, 1935-1940 (Boston: American Board of Commissioners for Foreign Missions).

Appendix D

Communicant Membership of the Episcopal Church

Year	Total Communicants	Active Members
1882	426 a	761 b
1887	728 a	1,300 c
1890	2,028 a	3,623
1904	7,205 a	12,867
1907	7,506 a	13,404
1910	8,095 a	14,202
1911	8,428 a	14,786
1912	8,916	15,373
1913	9,005	15,604
1915	9,769	17,091
1917	10,527	18,287
1923	11,455	19,700
1926	12,980	21,719
1927	13,473	22,235
1932	16,225	26,165
1937	18,195	28,859
1938	18,192	28,606

a. The figures for the years 1882 through 1911 are estimates derived from using the ratio found by comparing the number of total communicants to active members in the years 1912 to 1938. Matsudaira's "total communicants" is comparable to the communicant memberships of other churches used in this book. For the distinction between "total communicants" and "active members" refer to p. 4.

b. Taken from *The Tokyo Conference Report,* p. 991.

c. See Cary, *History of Christianity,* p. 191.

Source: Itaro Matsudaira, an official historian of the Episcopal Church in Japan, Letter to the writer (March 6, 1962).

Appendix E
Communicant Membership of the American Baptist Church

Year	Communicants	Year	Communicants
1873	8	1907	2,608
1874	8	1908	2,722
1875	15	1909	2,934
1876	42	1910	3,054
1877	45	1911	3,304
1878	66	1912	3,580
1879	76	1913	3,978
1880	133	1914	3,920
1881	185	1915	4,292
1882	239	1916	3,670
1883	286	1917	3,651
1884	367	1918	3,778
1885	433	1919	3,830
1886	519	1920	3,809
1887	770	1921	3,797
1888	900	1922	3,990
1889	905	1923	4,284
1890	1,056	1924	4,389
1891	1,170	1925	4,438
1892	1,337	1926	4,858
1893	1,565	1927	4,714
1894	1,633	1928	4,375
1895	1,533	1929	4,348
1896	1,586	1930	4,907
1897	1,619	1931	4,432
1898	1,601	1932	4,492
1899	1,885	1933	4,660
1900	2,011	1934	4,575
1901	2,213	1935	4,629
1902	2,157	1936	4,347
1903	2,151	1937	4,401
1904	2,219	1938	4,107
1905	2,110	1939	4,107
1906	2,347		

Source: American Baptist Foreign Mission Society, *Annual Reports*, 1874-1940 (Boston: Foreign Mission Rooms). The annuals up to 1909 are known as those of the American Baptist Missionary Union.

Appendix F

Communicant Membership of the Southern Baptist Church

Year	Communicants	Year	Communicants
1890	15	1915	694
1891	25	1916	756
1892	27	1917	930
1893	31	1918	994
1894	40	1919	1,084
1895	40	1920	1,048
1896	48	1921	1,238
1897	61	1922	1,355
1898	71	1923	1,717
1899	75	1924	1,511
1900	90	1925	1,978
1901	114	1926	2,185
1902	120	1927	2,349
1903	175	1928	2,467
1904	223	1929	2,515
1905	224	1930	2,630
1906	300	1931	2,722
1907	339	1932	2,803
1908	456	1933	2,686
1909	504	1934	2,814
1910	578	1935	2,671
1911	535	1936	2,781
1912	565	1937	2,642
1913	617	1938	2,776
1914	659	1939	2,776

Source: Southern Baptist Convention, *Annual of the Southern Baptist Convention,* 1891-1940 (Richmond, Va.: Foreign Mission Board, Southern Baptist Convention).

Appendix G
Communicant Membership of the Disciples of Christ

Year	Communicants	Year	Communicants
1889	168	1917	1,000
1897	368	1920	1,455
1898	484	1921	1,293
1899	611	1922	1,254
1900	734	1923	1,627
1901	679	1924	1,668
1902	684	1925	1,655
1903	992	1926	1,743
1904	1,119	1927	1,865
1905	859	1928	1,852
1906	1,085	1929	2,118
1907	1,194	1930	2,223
1908	1,396	1931	2,388
1909	1,500	1934	2,324
1911	1,691	1935	2,347
1912	1,654	1936	2,349
1913	1,827	1937	2,267
1914	1,387	1938	2,123
1915	966	1939	2,299

Source: Edwin M. Bliss (ed.), *The Encyclopaedia of Missions*, Vol. 2 (New York: Funk and Wagnalls, 1891), p. 610; Mrs. Maude Whitmore Madden, *The Churches of Christ Mission in Japan, 1883-1908* (a booklet); The Foreign Christian Missionary Society, *The Missionary Intelligencer*, 1912-1918 (Cincinnati, Ohio: The Foreign Christian Missionary Society); The United Christian Missionary Society, *Year Book of Churches of Christ, 1921-1940* (St. Louis: The United Christian Missionary Society).

Appendix H
Communicant Membership of the Seventh-Day Adventist Church

Year	Communicants	Year	Communicants
1897	13a	1923	376
1902	55	1924	425
1906	108	1925	460
1907	110	1926	502
1908	119	1927	548
1909	168	1928	596
1910	199	1929	673
1911	189	1930	741
1913	234	1931	763
1914	243	1932	824
1915	323	1933	906
1916	263a	1934	980
1918	324	1935	1,057
1919	305	1936	1,094
1920	286	1937	1,143
1921	299	1938	1,184
1922	323	1939	1,228

a. F.R. Millard, Letter to the writer (March 5, 1962).

Source: Seventh-Day Adventists, *Annual Statistical Reports of the General Conference of Seventh-Day Adventists*, 1903-1940 (Takoma Park, Washington, D.C.: General Conference of Seventh-Day Adventists).

Appendix I
Communicant Membership of the Holiness Church

Year	Communicants	Year	Communicants
1915	1,143a	1930	12,046a
1920	1,667b	1931	11,330a
1921	1,821b	1932	19,523a
1922	2,732b	1933	19,351a
1923	2,764b	1934	19,752c
1924	2,987a	1935	20,256c
1925	3,123a	1936	21,422c
1926	5,217b	1937	22,824c
1928	7,878a	1938	22,621c
1929	9,812a	1939	21,965c

a. Yoshiyasu Kami and Kunio Kato, Protesutanto Hyakunenshi Kenkyu (Tokyo: The Research Institute of the Mission, The United Church of Christ in Japan, 1961), pp. 110-117.

b. Isamu Yoneda, Nakada Jyuji Den (Tokyo: Nakada Jyuji Den Kando Kai, 1959), pp. 344, 381.

c. The Japan Holiness Church faced an internal problem which came to a head in September of 1933. The church was split into two factions, Holiness Church (Kiyome Kyokai) headed by Bishop Nakada and Japan Holiness Church (Nippon Sei Kyokai) led by the seminary professors. Therefore, the 1934 figure of 19,752 communicants must be understood as being 11,424 for the former group and 8,328 for the latter. The communicant figures for the subsequent years up to 1939 follow the same rule. See Kami and Kato, Protesutanto, pp. 110-117.

	Kiyome Kyokai	Nippon Sei Kyokai
(1935)	11,506	8,750
(1936)	12,407	9,015
(1937)	13,180	9,644
(1938)	13,909	8,712
(1939)	14,607	7,358

Notes

Introduction

1. The principle behind the methodology used here is no monopoly of this writer. What is commonly known as "church growth literature" adheres to it, whether it is explicitly stated or implied. A few notable examples are: Donald Anderson McGavran, *How Churches Grow* (London: World Dominion Press, 1959), Chapter XIX; Keith E. Hamilton, *Church Growth in the High Andes* (Lucknow, U. P., India: The Lucknow Publishing House, 1962); Roy E. Shearer, *Wildfire, Church Growth in Korea* (Grand Papids, Mich.: W. B. Eerdmans, 1966); John B. Brimley and Gordon E. Robinson, *Church Growth in Central and Southern Nigeria* (Grand Rapids, Mich.: W. B. Eerdmans, 1966); Alan R. Tippett, *Solomon Islands Christianity: A Study in Growth and Obstruction* (London: Lutterworth Press, 1967).

2. Stephen Neill, *The Christian Society* (London: Nisbet & Co., Ltd., 1952), pp. 296-298. The word "Church" is used to: (1) connote its "mystical sense" in which it is interpreted "as the body of Christ, the Bride, not having spot or wrinkle or any such thing, the Church as Christ intended it to be"; (2) "express the fellowship of all those who now or at any time are or have been of the company of the redeemed in Christ"; (3) "mean all those who at any one time in the world's history are within God's covenant of grace"; (4) "describe the group of Christians worshiping in a single place, and bound together by a common loyalty and an experience in common of the presence of Christ in worship"; (5) refer, beyond the local basis, to the Church of England, the Church of Sweden, and so forth; or (6) signify a denomination.

3. Lloyd Vernor Ballard, *Social Institutions* (New York: D. Appleton-Century Company, Inc., 1936), p. 441.

4. Earnest E. Best, *Christian Faith and Cultural Crisis, The Japanese Case* (Leiden: E. J. Brill, 1966), p. 69; also see Joachim Wach, *Sociology of Religion* (Chicago: The University of Chicago Press, 1944), Chapter II.

5. Eugene Nida, "Ideological Conflicts," Donald McGavran (ed.), *Church Growth and Christian Mission* (New York: Harper & Row, Publishers, 1965), p. 57.

6. Joseph H. Fichter, *Social Relations in the Urban Parish* (Chicago: The University of Chicago Press, 1954). The entire book is an illuminating discussion of the typology of religious participation on the basis of research conducted in urban Catholic parishes in the United States. He uses such categories as nuclear, modal, marginal, and dormant depicting the degrees of participation in the parish life.

7. James S. Dennis, Harlan P. Beach, and Charles H. Fahs (eds.), *World Atlas of Christian Missions* (New York: Student Volunteer Movement for Foreign Missions, 1911); Harlan P. Beach and Charles H. Fahs (eds.), *World Missionary Atlas* (New York: Institute of Social and Religious Research, 1925); Joseph I. Parker (ed.), *Interpretative Statistical Survey of the World Mission of the Christian Church* (New York: International Missionary Council, 1938).

8. The Reverend Itaro Matsudaira's letter (March 6, 1962) to the writer containing figures under these four headings from 1913 to 1960.

9. See E. J. Bingle (ed.), *World Christian Handbook* (London: World Dominion Press, 1957) and its subsequent editions.

10. The category "community" is an elastic one, because different denominations define their own "communities" in different ways and because the community itself fluctuates. In time of persecution, *community* will shrink much more than *communicants*. But while elastic, the category must be used for two reasons.

First, the total population consists not of adults but of adults and minors, parents and infants; the only figure for Christians which can truly be compared with total population is *community*. If in a population of 1000, there are 100 communicants, it is grossly misleading to say that Christians comprise one tenth of the population. The 100 communicants have at least another hundred dependents, so *Christians* comprise at least *two tenths* of the total population. In the case of Japan, it may be necessary to multiply the communicants by 2.3 in order to come up with the community figure. The reason for using the figure 2.3 is the following. The Protestant Episcopal Church in Japan has kept careful membership records under four headings for many years (as mentioned earlier): (1) Active Communicants; (2) Total Communicants; (3) Active Members; and (4) Total Members. The average "Total Members" *for the last forty years* is 2.3 times the average "Total Communicants." There is every reason to believe that the "Christian Communities" of the other major churches in Japan are very similar to the "Christian Community" (listed under Total Members) of the Seikokai; and that the ratio of their communicants or full members to their "Christian Communities" would be somewhat the same as its.

Second, since some denominations report only community (for example, the Roman Catholics) and some report only communicants (for example, the Baptists) when figures are *compared*, one must either transform communicants into community by multiplying by a carefully determined factor, or he must reduce community to communicants by dividing by that same factor. To report 17,000 members (communicants) for one denomination and 38,000 members (community) for another and let readers infer that denomination two is twice as large as denomination one is criminal carelessness. Granting that transforming communicants into community involves error, it is minor error compared with the major untruth of comparing incomparables.

11. The writer began by consulting inter-church sources such as *Encyclopaedia of Missions* (1891), *World Atlas of Christian Missions* (1911), *World Missionary Atlas* (1925), and *Interpretative Statistical Survey of the World Mission* (1938). Many histories of Christian mission in Japan were carefully examined. The complete files of *The Japan Christian Year Books* (1903-1940) and of *The International Review of Missions* from 1912 on were tapped. Membership records were obtained from all eight denominations. Church historians, both Japanese and American, were consulted. Government statistics on church membership were inspected.

World-wide missionary sources and government statistics were found less reliable than denominational. Confusion has been caused by some compilers of world-wide missionary statistics who have taken communicant figures for one survey and community figures for another. Episcopalian communicants given by world-wide sources, for example, should be compared with those given to the writer by the official historian, the Reverend Matsudaira. (See McGavran, ed., *Church Growth and Christian Mission*, pp. 165, 166.) Government statistics before World War II, on the other hand, were compiled by the Department of Home Affairs mainly for the purpose of religious and political control and showed, as a rule, much less than the figures claimed by various churches and other statistical sources, though there was no real consistency.

The figures given in *The Japan Christian Year Books* are generally regarded as more reliable, and the denominational figures used in this study closely correspond to them. The trends of growth by both sources resemble each other. Since the communicant figures before 1903 (when *The Japan Christian Year Book* began) were needed in constructing the graph, the writer used the figures of membership obtained at the denominational mission archives or supplied by their own church historians.

The graph thus constructed, the reader needs to keep in mind, shows the strength of the church which merged within its denominational family such as Presbyterian (1877), Episcopal (1887), and Methodist (1907) on the single line graph collectively as though forming one church even before its merger. This is done partly to reveal the continuity of the particular church throughout the period of this study and partly to enable the comparison of the growth of eight churches possible.

12. Figure 1 is constructed from the following sources: Itaro Matsudaira, the official historian of the Seikokai, Letter to the writer (March 6, 1962); James A. Cogswell, Letter to the writer (February 9, 1962); Cogswell, "A History of the work of the Japan Mission of the Presbyterian Church in the United States, 1885-1960" (Unpublished Th. D. dissertation, Union Theological Seminary, Richmond, Va., 1961); American Baptist Foreign Mission Society, *Annual Reports*, 1874-1940 (Boston: Foreign Missions Rooms); American Board of Commissioners for Foreign Missions, *Annual Reports*, 1881-1903, 1905-1918, 1920-1923, 1926-1928, 1930-1933, 1935-1940 (Boston: American Board of Commissioners for Foreign Missions); Methodist Episcopal Church, Missionary Society, *Annual Reports of the Missionary Society of the Methodist Episcopal Church*, 1884-1906 (New York: Missionary Society of the Methodist Episcopal Church); Methodist Episcopal Church, South, Board of Missions, *Annual Reports of the Board of Missions*, 1888-1906 (Nashville, Tenn.: Publishing House of the Methodist Episcopal Church, South); Methodist Church (Canada), *Annual Reports of the Missionary Society of the Methodist Church*, 1883-1906 (Toronto:

Methodist Mission Rooms); M. Dorothy Woodruff, then Research Librarian of the Board of Missions, the Methodist Episcopal Church, Letter to the writer (March 20, 1962); Edwin M. Bliss (ed.), *The Encyclopaedia of Missions*, Vol. 2 (New York: Funk and Wagnalls, 1891), p. 610; Mrs. Maude Whitmore Madden, *The Churches of Christ Mission in Japan, 1883-1908* (a booklet); The Foreign Christian Missionary Society, *The Missionary Intelligencer*, 1912-1918 (Cincinnati, Ohio: The Foreign Christian Missionary Society); The United Christian Missionary Society, *Year Book of Churches of Christ*, 1921-1940 (St. Louis: The United Christian Missionary Society); Southern Baptist Convention, *Annual of the Southern Baptist Convention*, 1891-1940 (Richmond, Va.: Foreign Mission Board, Southern Baptist Convention); F. R. Millard, then Associate Secretary of General Conference of the Seventh-Day Adventists, Letter to the writer (March 5, 1962); Seventh-Day Adventists, *Annual Statistical Reports of the General Conference of Seventh-Day Adventists*, 1903-1940 (Takoma Park, Washington, D. C.: General Conference of Seventh-Day Adventists).

13. Winburn T. Thomas, "A History of Protestant Christianity in Japan" (Ph. D. dessertation, Yale University, 1942) later published as *Protestant Beginnings in Japan, the First Three Decades, 1859-1889* (Tokyo and Rutland, Vermont: Charles E. Tuttle Company, 1959).

14. Edwin Luther Copeland, "The Crisis of Protestant Missions to Japan, 1889-1900" (Unpublished Ph. D. dissertation, Yale University, 1949).

15. Fujio Ikado, "The Middle Class and Japanese Protestantism: A Socio-Historical Study of Mission Problems, Especially in Relation to Mission Schools" (Unpublished B. D. thesis, The University of Chicago, 1958), pp. 31, 32.

16. *Ibid.*, p. 32.

Chapter I

1. *Sociology of Religion*, p. 31. Cf. Robert M. MacIver, *Society: Its Structure and Changes* (New York: Farrar & Rinehart, 1937), p. 48.

2. Ferdinand Töennies, *Fundamental Concepts of Sociology*, translated from *Gemeinschaft und Gesellschaft* (1887) by Charles P. Loomis (New York: American Book Co., 1940).

3. Talcott Parsons and Edward A. Shils (eds.), *Toward a General Theory of Action* (Cambridge, Mass.: Harvard University Press, 1951).

4. Yoshiharu Scott Matsumoto, *Contemporary Japan: The Individual and the Group* (Philadelphia: The American Philosophical Society, 1960), p. 8, citing from Florence R. Kluckhohn, "Dominant and Variant Value Orientations," Clyde Kluckhohn and Henry A. Murray (eds.), *Personality in Nature, Society and Culture* (New York: Houghton Mifflin, 1934), p. 351.

5. Calvin Schnucker and Yutaka Sato, *Noson Dendo Proguramu* (Tokyo: Kirisuto Shimbun-sha, 1962), p. 171.

6. Tadashi Fukutake, *Japanese Rural Society*, translated from *Nihon Noson Shakai Ron* (1964) by R. P. Dore (Tokyo, London, and New York: Oxford University Press, 1967), p. 39.

7. Matsumoto, *Contemporary Japan*, p. 11.

8. *Ibid.*, citing from G. B. Sanson, *The Western World and Japan* (New York: Alfred A. Knopf, 1951), p. 448.

9. R. P. Dore, *City Life in Japan: A Study of a Tokyo Ward* (Berkeley and Los Angeles: University of California Press, 1958), pp. 97-100.

10. Fukutake, *Japanese Rural Society*, p. 47.

11. Robert N. Bellah, *Tokugawa Religion: The Values of Pre-Industrial Japan* (Glencoe, Illinois: The Falcon's Wing Press, 1957), pp. 46, 47.

12. Changboh Chee, "Development of Sociology in Japan: A Study of Adaptation of Western Sociological Orientations into the Japanese Social Structure" (Unpublished Ph. D. dissertation, Duke University, 1959), p. 37.

13. Matsumoto, *Contemporary Japan*, p. 12.

14. Edwin O. Reischauer, *The United States and Japan*, 1957 rev. ed. (New York: The Viking Press, 1950), p. 136.

15. *Ibid.*, p. 137.

16. Dore, *City Life*, p. 106.

17. Fukutake, *Japanese Rural Society*, p. 45.

18. Archaeological data substantiate the "antiquity of some sort of hamlet." In the Meiji period (1868-1911) the term *buraku* (hamlet) was coined to identify the settlement the typical of which was composed of fifty farm families (but no more than a hundred even including non-farming families) and was made a sub-unit of the administrative unit of the village or town. Cf. Erwin H. Johnson, "Status Changes in Hamlet Structure Accompanying Modernization" (Chapter V), R. P. Dore (ed.), *Aspects of Social Change in Modern Japan* (Princeton, N. J.: Princeton University Press, 1967), pp. 153, 154; Fukutake, *Japanese Rural Society*, p. 82.

19. Johnson, "Status Changes," p. 162.

20. *Ibid.*, pp. 163-165.

21. Fukutake, *Japanese Rural Society*, p. 85.

22. Johnson, "Status Changes." p. 165.

23. Otoyori Tahara, "Class Differentiation of Farmers and Social Structure of Farming Communities in Postwar Japan." Paul Halmos (ed.), *Japanese Sociological Studies* (Keele, Staffordshire: The University of Keele, 1966), p. 55.

24. Fukutake, *Japanese Rural Society*, p. 86.

25. John F. Embree, *Suye Mura, a Japanese Village* (Chicago: University of Chicago Press, 1939), p. 172.

26. R. J. Smith, "The Japanese Rural Community: Norms, Sanctions, and Ostracism," *American Anthropologist*, 63, ii, pt. 1 (1961), 524.

27. Embree, *Suye Mura*, p. 171.

28. Smith, "The Japanese Rural Community." p. 527.

29. *Ibid.*

30. Reischauer, *The United States and Japan*, p. 81.

31. *Ibid.*

32. Best, *Christian Faith and Cultural Crisis*, pp. 3, 4.

33. Reischauer, *The United States and Japan*, p. 82.

34. *Ibid.*

35. *Ibid.*

36. Fukutake, *Japanese Rural Society*, p. 140.

37. Japanese National Commission for UNESCO (comp.), *Japan: Its Land, People and Culture* (Tokyo: Printing Bureau, Ministry of Finance, 1958), p. 163. The population increase in prewar Japan was as follows: 35 million (1873), 46 million (1903), 56 million (1920), and 73 million (1940). See G. C. Allen, *A Short Economic History of Modern Japan, 1867-1937* (London: George Allen & Unwin, 1946), p. 194.

38. John W. Bennett, "Japanese Economic Growth: Background for Social Change" (Chapter XIII), Dore (ed.), *Aspects of Social Change*, p. 418.

39. See Joseph Jennes, *A History of the Catholic Church in Japan* (Tokyo: Oriens Institute for Religious Research, 1959); C. R. Boxer, *The Christian Century in Japan, 1549-1650* (Berkeley and Los Angeles: University of California Press, 1967) with an extensive bibliography, pp. 503-517.

40. Joseph J. Spae, *Catholicism in Japan, A Sociological Study* (Tokyo: ISR Press, 1964), pp. 4-6.

41. *Ibid.*, pp. 5, 6.

42. James A. Cogswell, *Until the Day Dawn* (Nashville: Board of World Missions, Presbyterian Church U. S., 1957), p. 15.

43. Charles W. Iglehart, *A Century of Protestant Christianity in Japan* (Rutland, Vermont and Tokyo: Charles E. Tuttle Company, 1959), p. 41.

44. G. F. Verbeck, "History of Protestant Missions in Japan," *Proceedings of the General Conference of the Protestant Missionaries of Japan, Osaka, April, 1883* (Yokohama: R. Meiklejohn & Co., 1883), p. 25. Generally known as *Osaka Conference Report.*

45. Henry St. George Tucker, *The History of the Episcopal Church in Japan* (New York: Charles Scribner's Sons, 1938), p. 132.

46. Ernest W. Clement, *Christianity in Modern Japan* (Philadelphia: American Baptist Publication Society, 1905), p. 89.

47. James A. Cogswell, Letter to the writer (February 9, 1962).

48. Albertus Pieters, *Mission Problems in Japan, Theoretical and Practical* (New York: The Board of Publication, Reformed Church in America, 1912), p. 69.

49. *Ibid.*, p. 70.

50. S. W. Ryder, *A Historical-Educational Study of the Japan Mission of the Reformed Church in America* (New York: The York Printing Co., 1935), p. 115.

51. *Ibid.*

52. William Wynd, *Seventy Years in Japan: A Saga of Northern Baptists* (New York: The American Baptist Foreign Mission Society, c. 1943), p. 2.

53. American Baptist Foreign Mission Society, *Annual Report* (Boston: Foreign Mission Rooms, 1873), p. 89.

54. M. L. Gordon, *An American Missionary in Japan* (Boston and New York: Houghton, Mifflin and Company, 1892), p. 149.

55. Otis Cary, *A History of Christianity in Japan*, Vol. 2 (New York: Fleming H. Revell Company, 1909), p. 107.

56. Arva Colbert Floyd, "The Founding of the Japan Methodist Church" (Unpublished Ph. D. dissertation, Yale University, 1939), p. 56.

57. Clement, *Christianity in Modern Japan*, p. 84.

58. Floyd, "Japan Methodist Church," pp. 302, 303.

59. Clement, *Christianity in Modern Japan*, p. 84.

60. Eiichi Kudo, "Shodai Nihon Protesutanto no Shakaiso," *The Meiji-gakuin Ronso*, No. 30 (October, 1953), p. 104.

61. Eiichi Kudo, *Nihon Shakai to Protesutanto Dendo* (Tokyo: Nihon Kirisuto Kyodan Shuppan-bu, 1959), p. 19.

62. James Johnston (ed.), *Report of the Centenary Conference on the Protestant Missions of the World*, Vol. 1 (New York: Fleming H. Revell Company, 1888), p. 256.

63. Edwin M. Bliss (ed.), *The Encyclopaedia of Missions*, Vol. 1 (New York: Funk and Wagnalls, 1891), p. 494.

64. Kudo, *Nihon Shakai*, p. 89.

65. The following figures show the communicant memberships of five churches around 1881 and are found in the appendixes: Presbyterian (1,642), Congregational (881), and American Baptist (185) for 1881; Methodist (846) and Episcopal (426) for 1882 with the total of 3, 980. Hereafter refer to the appendixes for the communicant memberships of our eight churches through the years unless otherwise indicated.

66. Cary, *History of Christianity*, Vol. 2, p. 105.

67. After the Meiji Restoration, the former class distinctions were abolished. The feudal lords and court nobles were made *kazoku* (peerages), the *samurai shizoku (warrior-class),* and the peasant-artisan-merchant classes *heimin* (commoners).

68. Best, *Christian Faith and Cultural Crisis*, p. 99.

69. Kudo, *Nihon Shakai*, pp. 23, 24.

70. Ikado, "The Middle Class," p. 5.

71. Kudo, *Nihon Shakai*, p. 65.

72. *Ibid.*, pp. 146, 147. Though the ten-year period of rural receptivity goes beyond the limits of this chapter, the writer feels that the topic of the rural church as a whole may be more profitably discussed here.

73. Kudo, "Shodai Nihon," p. 111.

74. See Charles Y. Glock, "The Role of Deprivation in the Origin and Evolution of Religious Groups," Robert Lee and Martin Marty (eds.), *Religion and Social Conflict* (New York: Oxford University Press, 1964). And to give an even more basic reference, see Robert K. Merton's essay on relative deprivation in *Social Theory and Social Structure,*rev. and enlarged ed. (New York: The Free Press, 1967), pp. 227-236.

75. Masao Takenaka, *Reconciliation and Renewal in Japan* (New York: Friendship Press, 1957), pp. 17, 18.

76. Best, *Christian Faith and Cultural Crisis*, p. 96.

77. Bunnosuke Sekine, *Nihon Seishinshi to Kirisutokyo* (Osaka: Sogensha, 1962), pp. 69, 70.

78. Wynd, *Seventy Years*, p. 7.

79. Kiyomi Morioka, "Christianity in the Japanese Rural Community: Acceptance and Rejection," Paul Halmos (ed.), *Japanese Sociological Studies* (Keele, Staffordshire: University of Keele, 1966).

80. *Ibid.*, p. 189.

81. *Ibid.*, p. 186.

82. *Ibid.*, p. 187.

83. *Ibid.*, p. 189.

84. Fukutake, *Japanese Rural Society*, p. 140; Mikio Sumiya, *Kindai Nihon no Keisei to Kirisutokyo* (Tokyo: Shinkyo Shuppansha, 1961), p. 75.

85. Best, *Christian Faith and Cultural Crisis*, p. 80.

86. See Chapter III.

87. Best, *Christian Faith and Cultural Crisis*, pp. 81-85.

88. Kudo, *Nihon Shakai*, p. 180.

89. Ikado, "The Middle Class," p. 12; Pieters, *Mission Problems*, p. 120.

90. Chiyomatsu Katakozawa, *Nihon Shinkyo Hyakunen no Ayumi* (Tokyo: Nihon Y. W. C. A. Domei, 1957), p. 45.

91. Iglehart, *Protestant Christianity*, pp. 55, 56.

CHAPTER II

1. Herbert Passin, "The Sources of Protest in Japan," *American Political Science Review*, Vol. 56 (June, 1962), 397.

2. Delmer M. Brown, *Nationalism in Japan: An Introductory Historical Analysis* (Berkeley and Los Angeles: University of California Press, 1955), p. 111.

3. *Ibid.*, p. 104.

4. *Ibid.*, pp. 103, 104.

5. Iglehart, *Protestant Christianity*, p. 68.

6. Thomas, *Protestant Beginnings*, p. 171.

7. Kudo, *Nihon Shakai*, p. 184.

8. Iglehart, *Protestant Christianity*, p. 67.

9. *Ibid.*

10. Japanese National Commission for UNESCO (comp.), *Japan: Its Land, People and Culture*, p. 128.

11. Best, *Christian Faith and Cultural Crisis*, p. 15.

12. Japanese National Commission for UNESCO (comp.), *Japan*, p. 54.

13. Brown, *Nationalism in Japan*, p. 113.

14. Thomas, *Protestant Beginnings*, p. 57.

15. Best, *Christian Faith and Cultural Crisis*, p. 67.

16. *Ibid.*

17. *Ibid.*, p. 66.

18. Brown, *Nationalism in Japan*, p. 100.

19. Best, *Christian Faith and Cultural Crisis*, p. 67.

20. *Ibid.*

21. Kirisutokyo Gakko Kyoiku Domei (comp.), *Nihon ni Okeru Kirisutokyo Gakko Kyoiku no Genjo* (Tokyo: The Education Association of Christian Schools in Japan, 1961), p. 7.

22. Cary, *History of Christianity*, p. 164.

23. *Ibid.*

24. Archibald McLean, *The History of the Foreign Christian Missionary Society* (New York: Fleming H. Revell Company, 1919), pp. 91, 92.

25. *Ibid.*, p. 93.

26. Cogswell, *Until the Day Dawn*, p. 50, citing from *The Missionary* (May, 1885), p. 166.

27. *Ibid.*, p. 52.

28. Tosa was one of the strongholds of *outside clans* which overthrew the Tokugawa regime.

29. Cogswell, *Until the Day Dawn*, p. 54.

30. *Ibid.*, p. 55.

31. *Ibid.*

32. *Ibid.*, pp. 59, 60.

33. James Cannon, III, *History of Southern Methodist Missions* (Nashville, Tenn.: Cokesbury Press, 1926), pp. 131, 132.

34. *Ibid.*, p. 133.

35. Published in book form in 1959 under the title, *Protestant Beginnings in Japan, the First Three Decades, 1859-1889.*

36. *Ibid.*, p. 88.

37. *Ibid.*, p. 86, 87.

38. *Ibid.*, p. 87.

39. *Ibid.*

40. *Ibid.*, p. 172.

41. Iglehart, *Protestant Christianity*, p. 126.

42. *Ibid.*, p. 154, citing from Masaharu Anesaki, *History of Japanese Religion* (London: Kegan Paul, Trench, Trubner & Co., Ltd., 1930), p. 356.

43. *Ibid.*, p. 88.

44. *Ibid.*, p. 72.

45. *Ibid.*

46. Itaro Matsudaira, *Nihon Seikokai Hyakunenshi* (Tokyo: Nihon Seikokai Bunshokyoku, 1959), p. 96.

47. Thomas, *Protestant Beginnings*, p. 73.

48. *Ibid.*, p. 170.

49. *Ibid.*, p. 74.

50. *Ibid.*, p. 75.

51. *Ibid.*, p. 100.

52. *Ibid.*, p. 74.

53. *Ibid.*, p. 116.

54. *Ibid.*, p. 171.

55. *Ibid.*, p. 84.

56. *Ibid.*

57. Mutsuro Sugii, "Meiji Oyobi Taisho Zenhanki Nihon Protesutantism No Ichi Kosatsu." An unpublished manuscript of an analysis of the data presented in Keiseisha (ed.), *Shinkou Sanjunen Kirisutosha Retsuden* (Tokyo: Keiseisha, 1920).

58. *Ibid.*, p. 82.   59. Bliss (ed.), *Encyclopaedia of Missions*, p. 498.

60. Sugii's manuscript, pp. 23, 36, 37.

61. *Ibid.*, p. 23.

62. *Ibid.*, pp. 35, 36.

63. *Ibid.*, p. 37.

64. Best, *Christian Faith and Cultural Crisis*, p. 98. The mission schools concentrated on the education beyond the elementary grades.

65. Thomas, *Protestant Beginnings*, p. 172.

66. Sugii's manuscript, p. 56.

67. Donald McGavran uses this expression to describe the distinctive kind of church growth obtained in Rhodesia and Zambia. It is also appropriate for Japan. See Mc Gavran, *Understanding Church Growth* (Grand Rapids, Michigan: William B. Eerdmans Publishing Company, 1970), pp. 20-24.

68. Persons who were baptized shortly after their graduation.

69. Thomas, *Protestant Beginnings*, p. 84.

70. Sugii's manuscript, p. 58.

71. *Ibid.*

72. Gordon, *American Missionary*, p. 155.

73. Thomas, *Protestant Beginnings*, p. 74.

74. Robert Bruce Mutch, "Channing Moore Williams; First Anglican Bishop of Yedo" (Unpublished M. A. thesis, Columbia University, 1966), pp. 77. 78.

75. Clement, *Christianity in Modern Japan*, p. 59.

76. Iglehart, *Protestant Christianity*, p. 82.

77. T. A. Young, "Japan," W. R. Warren (ed.), *Survey of Service, Disciples of Christ* (St. Louis: Christian Board of Publication, 1928), p. 343.

78. Best, *Christian Faith and Cultural Crisis*, p. 46.

79. *Ibid.*, p. 47.

80. *Ibid.*, p. 99.

81. Iglehart, *Protestant Christianity*, p. 72.

82. *Ibid.*, p. 73.

83. Cary, *History of Christianity*, p. 171.

84. *Ibid.*

85. *Ibid.*, p. 172.

86. Iglehart, *Protestant Christianity*, p. 73.

CHAPTER III

1. Thomas, *Protestant Beginnings*, p. 202.

2. *Ibid.*, pp. 203, 204; Brown, *Nationalism in Japan*, p. 125.

3. Copeland, "The Crisis of Protestant Missions," p. 78.

4. Brown, *Nationalism in Japan*, p. 113.

5. Copeland, "The Crisis of Protestant Missions," p. 81.

6. *Ibid.*, p. 86.

7. Thomas, *Protestant Beginnings*, p. 13.

8. *Ibid.*, p. 64.

9. Copeland, "The Crisis of Protestant Missions," p. 87.

10. *Ibid.*, p. 88.

11. *Ibid.*, p. 89.

12. *Ibid.*

13. *Ibid.*, p. 90.

14. *Ibid.*

15. *Ibid.*

16. Cary, *History of Christianity*, p. 254.

17. *Ibid.*

18. Copeland, "The Crisis of Protestant Missions," p. 91.

19. *Ibid.*, pp. 91, 92.

20. *Ibid.*, p. 91.

21. *Ibid.*, p. 93.

22. *Ibid.*

23. Brown, *Nationalism in Japan*, p. 126.

24. *Ibid.*

25. McLean, *The History of the Foreign Christian Missionary Society*, p. 93.

26. Ikado, "The Middle Class," p. 61.

27. Mikio Sumiya, "The Modernization of Japan," Robert M. Fukada (ed.), *God's People in Asian Industrial Society* (Kyoto: Naigai Printing Company, 1967), p. 73.

28. *Ibid.*

29. *Ibid.*, p. 74.

30. *The Foreign Mission Journal*, Vol. XLVI, No. 6 (March, 1896), p. 5.

31. Norman Wade Cox (ed.), *Encyclopedia of Southern Baptists*, Vol. 1 (Nashville, Tenn.: Broadman Press, 1958), p. 697.

32. Morris J. Wright, "Survey and Growth Evaluation of the Japan Baptist Convention, 1950-1960" (D.R.E. dissertation, Southwestern Baptist Theological Seminary, 1961), p. 1.

33. Henry C. Vedder, *A Short History of Baptist Missions* (Philadelphia: The Judson Press, 1927), p. 239.

34. J. F. Love, *Southern Baptists and Their Far Eastern Missions* (Richmond, Va.: The Foreign Mission Board, Southern Baptist Convention, 1922), pp. 272, 273.

35. Cox (ed.), *Encyclopedia of Southern Baptists*, p. 697.

36. Emma Howell Cooper, *The Great Advent Movement* (Washington, D. C.: Review and Herald Publishing Association, 1935), p. 212.

37. Mahlon Ellsworth Olsen, *A History of the Progress of Seventh-Day Adventists* (Washington, D. C. : Review and Herald Publishing Association, 1925), p. 675; Don F. Neufeld (ed.), *Seventh-Day Adventist Encyclopedia* (Washington, D. C.: Review and Herald Publishing Association, 1966), p. 629.

38. Olsen, *History of Seventh-Day Adventists*, p. 679.

39. *Ibid*.

40. *Ibid*., p. 680.

41. Tucker, *History of the Episcopal Church*, p. 145.

42. Copeland, "The Crisis of Protestant Missions," p. 50.

43. *Ibid*., pp. 50, 51.

44. Pieters, *Mission Problems*, p. 66.

45. *Ibid*.

46. See *Tokyo Conference Report*, pp. 994, 995. Note the considerable decrease in the enrollments of middle school students in these two churches. Most student converts during this period came from this age bracket (12-18).

47. Brown, *Nationalism in Japan*, p. 120, citing from Inoue, *Kyoiku to Shukyo to no Shototsu* (Conflict Between Education and Religion), quoted in Sadao Kiyohara, *Meiji Jidai Shiso Shi* (Tokyo: Daitokaku, 1921), pp. 160, 161.

48. Ikado, "The Middle Class," p. 62.

49. Cogswell, *Until the Day Dawn*, p. 72.

50. Best, *Christian Faith and Cultural Crisis*, p. 151. It is an established fact among the Japanese church historians that the two largest churches, especially the Congregational Church, received into their memberships many from the upper class during the period of pro-Westernism prior to the granting of the Constitution. As we shall see in the following chapter, the period of the 1880's may be said to have been the only period in which Japanese Protestantism had any notable response whatsoever from the upper class. The change on the political scene quickly nullified the pragmatic reason for the people of the upper class to join or remain in the church. The Congregational Church showed a sharp decline soon after 1890. C.f. Sumiya, *Kindai Nihon*, pp. 92-94.

51. Robert E. Speer, *Report on the Japan Missions of the Presbyterian Board of Foreign Missions*, 2nd ed. (New York: The Board of Foreign Missions of the Presbyterian Church in the U. S. A., 1897), p. 17.

52. Copeland, "The Crisis of Protestant Missions," p. 64.

53. In giving reasons for this, Copeland wrote: "In the first place, their greater numerical strength made them more aware than smaller groups of their right to authority. Secondly, these two denominations, particularly the Kumiai Kyokai [Congregational Church], had a tradition of larger liberty in their ecclesiastical polity and in the missionaries' policies than was the case in the other churches. Thirdly, they had a much better trained and more capable native leadership than did the others. And lastly, in these two bodies, there were more congregations which were free from foreign financial aid." *Ibid*., pp. 64, 65.

54. *Ibid*., p. 66.

55. Yasuo Furuya, "A Review of the Role of Christianity in Japanese Thought," *The Japan Christian Year Book* (1968), p. 12.

56. Speer, *Report on the Japan Missions*, p. 17.

57. *Ibid*.

58. Cary, *History of Christianity*, p. 215.

59. *The Christian Movement in Its Relation to the New Life in Japan* (Yokohama, 1903) p. 63.

60. McGavran, *Understanding Church Growth*, p. 92.

61. Joseph J. Spae, *Christianity Encounters Japan* (Tokyo: Oriens Institute for Religious Research, 1968), p. 170.

62. *The Christian Movement in Japan* (1903), p. 63.

63. Those whom the writer interviewed gave this factor as having contributed to membership leakage. The reasons they gave made sense and are given below.

64. Cary, *History of Christianity*, p. 215.

65. Morioka, "Christianity in the Japanese Rural Community," Halmos (ed.), *Japanese Sociological Studies*, p. 194.

66. Eugene A. Nida, "Culture and Church Growth," *Practical Anthropology*, Vol. 12, No. 1 (January-February, 1965), 26.

CHAPTER IV

1. Scholars date the end of the Hard Line Period variously: 1896 (Brown), 1899 (Clement), and 1900 (Cary). But, by the beginning of this chapter (1903), the sharp edge of the wintry climate may surely be said

to have eased. See Arthur Judson Brown, *One Hundred Years* (New York: Fleming H.Revell Company, 1936), p. 695; Clement, *Christianity in Modern Japan* (1910), pp. 644, 645.

2. Copeland, "The Crisis of Protestant Missions," p. 314; *Missionary Herald*, May, 1901, p. 187; *The Christian Movement in Japan*, (1910), pp. 644, 645.

3. Copeland, "The Crisis of Protestant Missions," p. 315; *Tokyo Conference Report*, p. 526. One missionary report stated: "The Gospel finds a ready hearing. The sale of Bibles and Christian literature has been phenomenal. American Baptist Foreign Mission Rooms), p. 165.

4. Copeland, "The Crisis of Protestant Missions," p. 315; M. L. Gordon, "The Turning of the tide in Japan," November 10, 1897, American Board of Commissioners for Foreign Missions, Correspondence from Japan Mission, 1890-1899, Vol. II.

5. *The Japan Weekly Mail*, April 6, 1901, p. 368, cited in Copeland, "The Crisis of Protestant Missions," pp. 317, 318.

6. Japanese National Commission for UNESCO (comp.), *Japan*, p. 55.

7. Copeland, "The Crisis of Protestant Missions," p. 330.

8. *Ibid.*, pp. 324-326.

9. Mikio Sumiya, *Social Impact of Industrialization in Japan* (Tokyo: Printing Bureau, Ministry of finance, 1963), p. 58.

10. Japanese National Commission for UNESCO (comp.), *Japan*, p. 59.

11. Sumiya, *Social Impact of Industrialization*, p. 75.

12. *Ibid.*, p. 76.

13. Jitsuichi Masuoka, "Urbanization and the Family in Japan," *Sociology and Social Research*, Vol. 32 (1947-48), 537.

14. *Ibid.*, 538, 539.

15. Kudo, *Nihon Shakai*, pp. 194-197.

16. Sumiya, *Social Impact of Industrialization*, p. 78.

17. C. Wright Mills, *White Collar: The American Middle Classes* (New York: Oxford University Press, 1951), p. 65.

18. Japanese National Commission for UNESCO (comp.), *Japan*, p. 409.

19. Best, *Christian Faith and Cultural Crisis*, p. 134.

20. Sumiya, *Social Impact of Industrialization*, p. 77. The productive age was set between fifteen and fifty-four.

21. Pieters, *Mission Problems*, p. 120.

22. Galen M. Fisher, "The Missionary Significance of the Last Ten Years: A Survey," *The International Review of Missions*, Vol. II (April, 1922) , 204.

23. *Ibid.*

24. Theodore Jaeckel, "Japan's Spiritual Situation," *The Japan Christian Quarterly*, Vol. XXI, No. 3 (July 1955), p. 195.

25. Ikado, "The Middle Class," p. 57.

26. See Table 17, "Marital Status and Sex Distribution," p. 124.

27. Copeland, "The Crisis of Protestant Missions," p. 317

28. The American Baptist Church increased by 1,627, the Southern Baptist by 820, and the Seventh-Day Adventist by 269.

29. Iglehart, *Protestant Christianity*, p. 119.

30. Kudo, *Nihon Shakai*, p. 232.

31. Masao Takenaka, "Relation of Protestantism to Social Problems in Japan, 1900-1941" (Unpublished Ph. D. dissertation, Yale University, 1954), p. 156, citing Cary, *History of Christianity*, p. 299.

32. Kudo, *Nihon Shakai*, pp. 229, 230.

33. Cary, *History of Christianity*, p. 304.

34. Zenkoku Kyodo Dendo Iin (ed.), *San-nen Keizoku Zenkoku Kyodo Dendo* (Tokyo: Fukuin Insatsu Co., Ltd., 1918), p. 62.

35. Takenaka, "Relation of Protestantism," p. 156.

36. D. R. McKenzie, "National Evangelistic Campaign," *The Christian Movement in Japan* (1917), p. 196.

37. Iglehart, *Protestant Christianity*, p. 121.

38. *Ibid.*

39. McKenzie, "National Evangelistic Campaign," p. 196.

40. American Board of Commissioners for Foreign Missions, *Annual Report*, 1907 (Boston: American Board of Commissioners for Foreign Missions), p. 136.

41. The Seventh-Day Adventist figures are absent from the table due to incomplete statistics.

42. See pp. 78-82.

43. McGavran, *Understanding Church Growth*, p. 140

44. Best, *Christian Faith and Cultural Crisis*, p. 146.

45. *Ibid.*

46. Refer to pp. 37-38.

47. See the extended analyses of the family system and the hamlet structure given in Chapter I (pp. 27-40).

48. James R. McGovern, "American Christian Missions to Japan, 1918-1941" (Unpublished Ph.D. dissertation, University of Pennsylvania, 1957), p. 146.

49. *Ibid.*, p. 151; C. M. Warren, "The Unreached in the Country and the Gospel Message," *Japan Evangelist*, XXIX (September, 1922), 256.

50. K. L. Butterfield, *The Rural Mission of the Church in East Asia* (New York: International Missionary Council, 1931), p. 113; McGovern, "American Christian Missions," p. 151.

51. *Ibid.*, p. 159.

52. Sumiya, "The Modernization of Japan," Fukada (ed.), *God's People in Asian Industrial Society*, p. 75.

53. Bruno Lasker, *Japan in Jeopardy* (New York: American Council, Institute of Pacific Relations, 1937), p. 15.

54. Yasuo Furuya, "A Review of the Role of Christianity in Japanese thought," *The Japan Christian Year Book*, 1968, p. 14; Ikado. "The Middle Class," p. 30.

55. Best, *Christian Faith and Cultural Crisis*, p. 146.

56. Keiichi Kobayashi, Eiichiro Ishii, and Fusao Nakajima, *Tokyo-kyoku Kyosei-no Jittai Chosa-o Chushintoshita Kosatsu* (Tokyo: The Research Institute of the Mission of the Church, United Church of Christ in Japan, 1961), pp. 74, 75.

57. Kudo, *Nihon Shakai*, p. 232.

58. Matsumoto, *Contemporary Japan*, p. 66.

59. Delmer Brown, "Speaking to the New Era: Christians Examine the Future (Christianity and Nationalism)," *The Japan Christian Year Book* (1968), p. 119.

60. Matsumoto, *Contemporary Japan*, p. 66.

61. Sumiya, "The Modernization of Japan," Fukada (ed.), *God's People in Asian Industrial Society*, p. 75.

62. Since this chapter deals primarily with the period 1903-1918, our discussion of the gulf should be limited to that period. But, because of the widening nature of the gulf which extends beyond 1918 to 1939, the writer judges that a fruitful exposition of the topic should encompass the entire spectrum.

63. Cogswell, *Until the Day Dawn*, p. 122.

65. Hiromichi Kozaki, *Kozaki Zenshu*, Vol. II (Tokyo: Kozaki Zenshu Kanko-kai, 1938), pp. 582, 583; The Japan Baptist Convention, *The History of Japan Baptist Convention, 1889-1959* (Tokyo: The Japan Baptist Convention, 1959), p. 429.

66. Clement, *Christianity in Modern Japan*, p. 92.

67. Commission on Christian Education in Japan, *Christian Education in Japan* (New York: The International Missionary Council, 1932), p. 148.

CHAPTER V

1. "The Missionary Significance of the Last Ten Years: A Survey," *The International Review of Missions*, Vol. 21 (1932), p. 21.

2. Reischauer, *The United States and Japan*, p. 191.

3. Cogswell, *Until the Day Dawn*, pp. 117, 118.

4. Reischauer, *The United States and Japan*, pp. 191, 192.

5. *Ibid.*, p. 192.

6. Cogswell, *Until the Day Dawn*, p. 116.

7. *Ibid.*, p. 118.

8. Arthur E. Tiedemann, *Modern Japan: A Brief History* (New York: D. Van Nostrand Company, Inc., 1955), p. 65.

9. Japan National Commission for UNESCO (comp.), *Japan*, p. 65.

10. Cogswell, *Until the Day Dawn*, p. 119.

11. *Ibid.*, p. 140.

12. McGovern, "American Christian Mission," p. 64.

13. Except for the sharp rise in 1936, the Congregational Church leveled off after 1930. The 1936 increase in membership was due to the absorption of the members of the Kurisuchian Kyokai (Christian Church) into the Congregational figure by merger. Though these two churches officially united in 1930 following the union of the parent bodies in America, the membership was not reported jointly till later.

The Christian Church mentioned here must not be confused with the Disciples of Christ. It was originally a split off from the Methodist Church in America during the nineteenth century and began its missionary work in Japan in 1887.

14. For example, Dr. Winburn Thomas, a former Presbyterian missionary to Japan, helps explain why the Congregational Church, which had such a virile beginning, stopped growing after 1930. Or, to put it

another way, the Presbyterian and Congregational Churches, whose growth patterns were closely parallel till about 1903, gradually drew apart, and by 1937 the Presbyterians had 20,000 more communicants than the Congregationalists. Thomas gives the reasons as to what caused this difference after carefully studying the writer's graph of growth, "How Eight Churches Grew in Japan" (Figure 1, p. 6). He wrote: "My suggested explanations for the Kumiai plateau after 1930, as over against the Nihon Kirisuto Kyokai's continued growth would be: (1) The liberal theological victory in the Congregational camp . . . cut the nerve of evangelistic activity. (2) Whereas Christian schools had been and continued to be the major source of new members, the Doshisha after that time was able to show relatively few converts. My wife was a professor at the Doshisha [during] 1931-40, and this subject was constantly being discussed. Whereas the Presbyterian Wilmina Jo-gakko in Osaka produced a large number of converts each year, Mrs. Thomas' own activity in the Doshisha Women's College was not equally productive. (3) After the revival of the Japanese spirit from 1933 onward, whereas the more rigidly neo-orthodox Nihon Kirisuto Kyokai continued to stress the fundamentals, the liberal Kumiai effort was short-circuited into political activity. The latter activity did not produce Christian converts." (Winburn T. Thomas, Letter to Donald A. McGavran, March 19, 1962.)

15. The sharp drop in 1934 is obviously due to a roll revision as evidenced by the subsequent continued growth.

16. See Tables 9-11 (pp. 105-107)

17. Charles W. Iglehart, "The Churches in 1931," *The Japan Christian Year Book* (1932), p. 74.

18. Takenada, "Relation of Protestantism," p. 205, citing from Shun-ichi Yokoyama, *Kagawa Toyohiko Den* (Biography of Toyohiko Kagawa), Tokyo, 1951, p. 318.

19. Iglehart, *Protestant Christianity*, p. 198.

20. McGovern, "American Christian Missions," p. 40.

21. S. M. Erickson, "The Problem of Rural Evangelization ," *The Christian Movement in Japan and Formosa* (1927), p. 52.

22. McGovern, "American Christian Missions," pp. 262, 263.

23. Iglehart, *Protestant Christianity*, p. 199.

25. Isamu Yoneda, *Nakada Jyuji Den* (Tokyo: Nakada Jyuji Den Kanko Kai, 1959), pp. 3-250.

26. *Ibid.*, pp. 470, 471; *The Japan Christian Year Book* (1938), p. 118.

27. Iglehart, "The Churches in 1931," *The Japan Christian Year Book* (1932), p. 75.

28. For the sake of brevity, the term "Kyodan" is used here to designate the "United Church of Christ in Japan" (Nippon Kirisuto Kyodan).

29. It is further assumed that the postwar social structure of the congregation is essentially similar to that which existed in prewar days. This assumption has been supported by approximately fifty pastors, missionaries, and laymen whom the writer interviewed. They were knowledgeable of the prewar situation.

30. Tooru Takakura (ed.), *Nihon Kirisutokyodan Nenkan* (Tokyo: the Publication Department of the United Church of Christ in Japan, 1968). The statistics given in it are for 1967.

31. E. H. Cressy, *Urban Growth in Tokyo* (Claremont, Calif.: E. H. Cressy, 1959), p. 4.

32. See Table 17 (p. 124).

33. This interview was arranged by Dr. Ryozo Hara of the Research Institute of the United Church of Christ in Japan. It took place in the home of Rev. Tosaji Obara in Tokyo on February 14, 1969. Accompanied by Dr. Hara, the writer had a unique opportunity to interview Rev. Akiji Kurumada, Rev. Yutaka Yoneda, and Rev. Tosaji Obara who made up the committee of three acting as bishops at the time of the 1936 division of the Holiness Church.

34. Yoneda, *Nakada Jyuiji Den*, p. 303.

35. *Ibid.*, pp. 418-429.

36. *Ibid.*, pp. 136, 137.

37. R. Kenneth Strachan, *The Inescapable Calling* (Grand Rapids, Michigan: William B. Eerdmans Publishing Company, 1968), p. 108.

38. Zenta Watanabe, *Kaishin To Sono Zengo* (Tokyo: The Publication Department of the United Church of Christ in Japan, 1957), p. 161.

39. Yoneda, *Nakada Jyuji Den*, p. 384.

The Soka Gakkai

1. Robert Lee constructed the table on the basis of figures given in *Religious Yearbooks* published by Ministry of Education, Tokyo. See *Stranger in the Land* (London: Lutterworth Press, 1967), p. 136.

2. Accurate Soka Gakkai figures are difficult to obtain. All figures relating to the membership of the Soka Gakkai are approximations since the Soka Gakkai reports its membership statistics in terms of family units. In order to convert household membership figures into actual membership figures, the number of family units must be "multiplied by three, as the figure for an average family." (See Lee, *Stranger in the Land*, p. 136.) The household membership for 1968 is reported as 6,618,000. When this figure is multiplied

by three, we arrive at the actual membership of 19,854,000 for the same year. See James Allen Dator, *Soka Gakkai, Builders of the Third Civilization* (Seattle & London: University of Washington Press, 1969), p. 61.

3. Yoshimitsu Endo, "Soka Gakkai, the Study of a Society for the Creation of Value," *Anglican Theological Review*, Vol. 46, No. 2 (April 1964), p. 137. For further explanation, see Noah Brannen, "Soka Gakkai's Theory of Value: An Analysis," *Contemporary Religions in Japan*, Vol. 5, No. 2 (June 1964), pp. 143-154.

4. Nichiren Shoshu, *Doctrines of Nichiren Shoshu* (Tokyo: Soka Gakkai Headquarters, 1957), p. 4.

5. Noah Brannen, "The Teachings of Soka Gakkai," *Contemporary Religions in Japan* Vol. 3, No. 3 (September 1962), pp. 258, 259.

6. *Ibid.*, p. 261.

7. Japan's quick economic recovery from the near devastation caused by World War II is often viewed as a modern miracle. Its record-breaking economic boom has visited many a Japanese with a gracious smile. It has brought prosperity to millions of "white-collared 'salary men,' businessmen and enterprising younger people" (see *Look*, September 10, 1963, p. 15). Yet, there are untold other millions who have been bypassed by this economic prosperity. They find their satisfaction elsewhere. Often they turn to one of the new religions to "find themselves."
The Soka Gakkai attracted its membership from the ranks of the disinherited. They are the "small businessmen and merchants, together with their employees, who are deprived of their share of prosperity and favorable living conditions" (see Endo, "Soka Gakkai," p. 133). Dator confirms the point by saying: "The several surveys we reviewed led us to conclude that typical members were, rather, of low (but not the lowest) socioeconomic status, their educational attainments and incomes were low, and they were generally in labor, artisan, or small shop occupations" (see Dator, *Soka Gakkai*, p. 132).

8. Werner Kohler, *Die Lotus-Lehre: Und Die Modernen Religionen in Japan* (Zurich: Atlantis Verlag, 1962).

9. James Allen Dator, "The Soka Gakkai: A Socio-Political Interpretation," *Contemporary Religions in Japan*, Vol. 6, No. 3 (September 1965), p. 221.

10. The success of the Soka Gakkai, according to David J. Hesselgrave, is largely due to its effective use of small groups. See "Soka Gakkai's Inner Thrust," *Evangelical Missions Quarterly*, Vol. 3, No. 3 (Spring 1967), pp. 129-136.

11. Dator, "The Soka Gakkai," pp. 223, 224.

12. *Ibid.*, pp. 225, 226.

13. *Ibid.*, p. 214. Also Dator, *"Soka Gakkai"* p. 6; G. B. Offner and H. Van Straelen, *Modern Japanese Religions* (New York: Twayne Publishers, Inc., 1963), p. 103.

14. Dator, "The Soka Gakkai," p. 215.

15. *Ibid.*, p. 213.

16. Lee, *Stranger in the Land*, p. 142.

17. *Ibid.*, p. 150.

18. Dator, *Soka Gakkai*, p. 84.

Selected Bibliography

Books

Allen, G.C. *A Short Economic History of Modern Japan, 1867-1937*. London: George Allen and Unwin, 1946.

American Baptist Foreign Mission Society. *Annual Reports, 1873-1940* (Boston: Foreign Mission Rooms).

American Board of Commissioners for Foreign Missions. *Annual Reports*, 1881-1903, 1905-1918, 1920-1923, 1926-1928, 1930-1933, 1935-1940 (Boston: American Board of Commissioners for Foreign Missions).

Anesaki, Masaharu. *History of Japanese Religion*. London: Kegan Paul, Trench, Trubner and Co., Ltd., 1930.

Ballard, Lloyd Vernor. *Social Institutions*. New York: D. Appleton-Century Company, Inc., 1936.

Beach, Harlan P., and Charles H. Fahs. (eds.). *World Missionary Atlas*. New York: Institute of Social and Religious Research, 1925.

Bellah, Robert N. *Tokugawa Religion: The Values of Pre-Industrial Japan*. Glencoe, Illinois: The Falcon's Wing Press, 1957.

Bennett, John W. "Japanese Economic Growth: Background for Social Change," R.P. Dore (ed.), *Aspects of Social Change in Modern Japan*. Princeton, N.J.: Princeton University Press, 1967.

Best, Earnest E. *Christian Faith and Cultural Crisis, The Japanese Case.* Leiden: E.J. Brill, 1966.

Bingle, E.J. (ed.). *World Christian Handbook.* London: World Dominion Press, 1957.

Bliss, Edwin M. (ed.). *The Encyclopaedia of Missions.* Vols. 1,2. New York: Funk and Wagnalls, 1891.

Boxer, C.R. *The Christian Century in Japan,* 1549-1650. Berkeley and Los Angeles: University of California Press, 1967.

Brimley, John B., and Gordon E. Robinson. *Church Growth in Central and Southern Nigeria.* Grand Rapids, Mich.: W.B. Eerdmans, 1966.

Brown, Arthur Judson. *One Hundred Years.* New York: Fleming H. Revell Company, 1936.

Brown, Delmer M. *Nationalism in Japan: An Introductory Historical Analysis.* Berkeley and Los Angeles: University of California Press, 1955.

Butterfield, K.L. *The Rural Mission of the Church in East Asia.* New York: International Missionary Council, 1931.

Cannon, James, III. *History of Southern Methodist Missions.* Nashville, Tenn.: Cokesbury Press, 1926.

Cary, Otis. *A History of Christianity in Japan.* Vol. 2. New York: Fleming H. Revell Company, 1909.

Clement, Ernest W. *Christianity in Modern Japan.* Philadelphia: American Baptist Publication Society, 1905.

Cogswell, James A. *Until the Day Dawn.* Nashville: Board of World Missions, Presbyterian Church U.S., 1957.

Commission on Christian Education in Japan. *Christian Education in Japan.* New York: The International Missionary Council, 1932.

Cooper, Emma Howell. *The Great Advent Movement.* Washington, D.C.: Review and Herald Publishing Association, 1935.

Cox, Noman Wade. (ed.). *Encyclopedia of Southern Baptists.* Vol. 1. Nashville, Tenn.: Broadman Press, 1958.

Cressy, E.H. *Urban Growth in Tokyo.* Claremont, Calif.: E. H. Cressy, 1959.

Dennis, James S., Harlan P. Beach, and Charles H. Fahs, (eds.). *World Atlas of Christian Missions.* New York: Student Volunteer Movement for Foreign Missions, 1911.

Dore, R.P. *City Life in Japan: A Study of a Tokyo Ward.* Berkeley and Los Angeles: University of California Press, 1958.

Embree, John F. *Suye Mura, a Japanese Village.* Chicago: University of Chicago Press, 1939.

Fichter, Joseph H. *Social Relations in the Urban Parish.* Chicago: University of Chicago Press, 1954.

Foreign Christian Missionary Society, The. *The Missionary Intelligencer,* 1912-1918 (Cincinnati, Ohio: The Foreign Christian Missionary Society).

Foreign Mission Journal, The. Vol. XLVI. No. 6 (March, 1896).

Fukutake, Tadashi. *Japanese Rural Society,* translated from *Nihon Noson Shakai Ron* by R.P. Dore. Tokyo: Kirisuto Shimbun-sha, 1962.

Glock, Charles Y. "The Role of Deprivation in the Origin and Evolution of Religious Groups," Robert Lee and Martin Marty (eds.), *Religion and Social Conflict.* New York: Oxford University Press, 1964.

Gordon, M.L. *An American Missionary in Japan.* Boston and New York: Houghton, Mifflin and Company, 1892.

Hamilton, Keith E. *Church Growth in the High Andes.* Lucknow, U.P., India: The Lucknow Publishing House, 1962.

Iglehart, Charles W. *A Century of Protestant Christianity in Japan.* Rutland, Vermont and Tokyo: Charles E. Tuttle Company, 1959.

Japan Baptist Convention, The. *The History of Japan Baptist Convention, 1889-1959.* Tokyo: The Japan Baptist Convention, 1959.

Japan Christian Year Book, The (Yokohama, 1903-1904, Tokyo, various publishers, 1905-1940). Title varies. The annual began first as *The Christian Movement in Its Relation to the New Life in Japan.*

Japan Weekly Mail, The (Yokohama, 1901). Weekly edition of *The Japan Daily Mail.*

Japanese National Commission for UNESCO (comp.). *Japan: Its Land, People and Culture.* Tokyo: Printing Bureau, Ministry of Finance, 1958.

Jennes, Joseph. *A History of the Catholic Church in Japan.* Tokyo: Oriens Institute for Religious Research, 1959.

Johnson, Erwin H. "Status Changes in Hamlet Structure AccompanyingModernization," R.P. Dore (ed.), *Aspects of Social Change in Modern Japan.* Princeton, N.J.: Princeton University Press, 1967.

Johnston, James. (ed.). *Report of the Centenary Conference on the Protestant Missions of the World.* Vol. 1. New York: Fleming H. Revell Company, 1888.

Katakozawa, Chiyomatsu. *Nihon Shinkyo Hyakunen no Ayumi* (A Centennial History of Japanese Protestantism). Tokyo: Nihon Y.W.C.A. Domei, 1957.

Keiseisha. (ed.). *Shinkou Sanjunen Kirisutosha Retsuden* (Brief Biographical Sketches of People with Thirty Years of Christian Life). Tokyo: Keiseisha, 1920.

Kirisutokyo Gakko Kyoiku Domei. (comp.). *Nihon ni Okeru Kirisutokyo Gakko Kyoiku no Genjo* (The Present Situation of the Work of the Christian Schools in Japan). Tokyo: The Education Association of Christian Schools in Japan, 1961.

Kiyohara, Sadao. *Meiji Jidai Shiso Shi* (History of Thought in the Meiji Era). Tokyo: Daitokaku, 1921.

Kluckhohn, Florence R. "Dominant and Variant Value Orientations," Clyde Kluckhohn and Henry A. Murray (eds.), *Personality in Nature, Society and Culture.* New York: Houghton Mifflin, 1934.

Kobayashi, Keiichi, Eiichiro Ishii, and Fusao Nakajima. *Tokyo-kyoku Kyosei-no Jittai Chosa-o Chushintoshita Kosatsu* (A Study of Church Growth on the Basis of the Survey Conducted in the Tokyo District). Tokyo: The Research Institute of the Mission of the Church, United Church of Christ in Japan, 1961.

Kozaki, Hiromichi, *Kozaki Zenshu* (Complete Works of Kozaki). Vol. 2 Tokyo: Kozaki Zenshu Kanko-kai, 1938.

Kudo, Eiichi. *Nihon Shakai to Purotesutanto Dendo* (Japanese Society and Protestant Missions). Tokyo: Nihon Kirisuto Kyodan Shuppan-bu, 1959.

Lasker, Bruno. *Japan in Jeopardy*. New York: American Council, Institute of Pacific Relations, 1937.

Love, J.F. *Southern Baptists and Their Far Eastern Missions*. Richmond, Va.: The Foreign Mission Board, Southern Baptist Convention, 1922.

MacIver, Robert M. *Society: Its Structure and Changes*. New York: Farrar and Rinehart, 1937.

McGavran, Donald. (ed.). *Church Growth and Christian Mission*. New York: Harper and Row, Publishers, 1965.

_____. *How Churches Grow*. London: World Dominion Press, 1959.

_____. *Understanding Church Growth*. Grand Rapids, Michigan: William B. Eerdmans Publishing Company, 1970.

McLean, Archibald. *The History of the Foreign Christian Missionary Society*. New York: Fleming H. Revell Company, 1919.

Madden, Mrs. Maude Whitmore. *The Churches of Christ Mission in Japan, 1883-1908*. A booklet.

Matsudaira, Itaro. *Nihon Seikokai Hyakunenshi* (One Hundred Years of the Episcopal Church in Japan). Tokyo: Nihon Seikokai Bunshokyoku, 1959.

Matsumoto, Yoshiharu Scott. *Contemporary Japan: The Individual and the Group*. Philadelphia: The American Philosophical Society, 1960.

Merton, Robert K. *Social Theory and Social Structure*. rev. and enlarged ed. New York: The Free Press, 1967.

Methodist Church (Canada). *Annual Reports of the Missionary Society of the Methodist Church, 1883-1906* (Toronto: Methodist Mission Rooms).

Methodist Episcopal Church, Missionary Society. *Annual Reports of the Missionary Society of the Methodist Episcopal Church, 1884-1906* (New York: Missionary Society of the Methodist Church).

Methodist Episcopal Church, South, Board of Missions. *Annual Reports of the Board of Missions,* 1888-1906 (Nashville, Tenn.: Publishing House of the Methodist Episcopal Church, South).

Mills, C. Wright. *White Collar: The American Middle Classes.* New York: Oxford University Press, 1951.

Morioka, Kiyomi. "Christianity in the Japanese Rural Community: Acceptance and Rejection," Paul Halmos (ed.), *Japanese Sociological Studies.* Keele, Staffordshire: University of Keele, 1966.

Neill, Stephen. *The Christian Society.* London: Nisbet and Co., Ltd., 1952.

Neufeld, Don F. (ed.). *Seventh-Day Adventist Encyclopedia.* Washington, D.C.: Review and Herald Publishing Association, 1966.

Olsen, Mahlon Ellsworth. *A History of the Progress of Seventh-Day Adventists.* Washington, D.C.: Review and Herald Publishing Association, 1925.

Parker, Joseph I. (ed.). *Interpretative Statistical Survey of the World Mission of the Christian Church.* New York: International Missionary Council, 1938.

Parsons, Talcott, and Edward A. Shils. (eds.). *Toward a General Theory of Action.* Cambridge, Mass.: Harvard University Press, 1951.

Pieters, Albertus. *Mission Problems in Japan, Theoretical and Practical.* New York: The Board of Publication, Reformed Church in America, 1912.

Proceedings of the General Conference of Protestant Missionaries in Japan, Tokyo, October, 1900. Tokyo: Methodist Publishing House, 1901.

Reischauer, Edwin O. *The United States and Japan.* 1957 rev. ed. New York: The Viking Press. 1950.

Ryder, S.W. *A Historical-Educational Study of the Japan Mission of the Reformed Church in America.* New York: The York Printing Co., 1935.

Sanson, G.B. *The Western World and Japan.* New York: Alfred A. Knopf, 1951.

Schnucker, Calvin, and Yutaka Sato. *Noson Dendo Proguramu* (The Program for Rural Evangelism). Tokyo: Kirisuto Shimbun-sha, 1962.

Sekine, Bunnosuke. *Nihon Seishinshi to Kirisutokyo* (Japan's Spiritual History and Christianity). Osaka: Sogensha, 1962.

Seventh-Day Adventists. *Annual Statistical Reports of the General Conference of Seventh-Day Adventists,* 1903-1940 (Takoma Park, Washington, D.C.: General Conference of Seventh-Day Adventists).

Shearer, Roy E. *Wildfire, Church Growth in Korea.* Grand Rapids, Mich.: W.B. Eerdmans, 1966.

Southern Baptist Convention. *Annual of the Southern Baptist Convention,* 1891-1940 (Richmond, Va.: Foreign Mission Board, Southern Baptist Convention).

Spae, Joseph J. *Catholicism in Japan, A Sociological Study,* Tokyo: ISR Press, 1964.

_____. *Christianity Encounters Japan.* Tokyo: Oriens Institute for Religious Research, 1968.

Speer, Robert E. *Report on the Japan Missions of the Presbyterian Board of Foreign Missions.* 2nd ed. New York: The Board of Foreign Missions of the Presbyterian Church in the U.S.A., 1897.

Strachan, R. Kenneth. *The Inescapable Calling.* Grand Rapids, Michigan: William B. Eerdmans Publishing Company, 1968.

Sumiya, Mikio. *Kindai Nihon no Keisei to Kirisutokyo* (The Formation of Modern Japan and Christianity). Tokyo: Shinkyo Shuppan-sha, 1961.

_____. *Social Impact of Industrialization in Japan.* Tokyo: Printing Bureau, Ministry of Finance, 1963.

_____. "The Modernization of Japan," Robert M. Fukada (ed.), *God's People in Asian Industrial Society.* Kyoto: Naigai Printing Company, 1967.

Tahara, Otoyori. "Class Differentiation of Farmers and Social Structure of Farming Communities in Postwar Japan," Paul Halmos (ed.), *Japanese Sociological Studies.* Keele, Staffordshire: The University of Keele, 1966.

Takakura, Tooru. (ed.). *Nihon Kirisutokyodan Nenkan* (The Annual of the United Church of Christ in Japan). Tokyo: The Publication Department of the United Church of Christ in Japan, 1968.

Takenaka, Masao. *Reconciliation and Renewal in Japan*. New York: Friendship Press, 1957.

Thomas, Winburn T. *Protestant Beginnings in Japan, the First Three Decades, 1859-1889*. Rutlan, Vermont: Charles E. Tuttle Company, 1959.

Tiedemann, Arthur E. *Modern Japan: A Brief History*. New York: D. Van Nostrand Company, Inc., 1955.

Tippett, Alan R. *Solomon Islands Christianity: A Study in Growth and Obstruction*. London: Lutterworth Press, 1967.

Töennies, Ferdinand. *Fundamental Concepts of Sociology*, translated from *Gemeinshaft und Gesselschaft* (1887) by Charles P. Loomis. New York: American Book Co., 1940.

Tucker, Henry St. George. *The History of the Episcopal Church in Japan*. New York: Charles Scribner's Sons, 1938.

United Christian Missionary Society, The. *Year Book of Churches of Christ, 1921-1940* (St. Louis: The United Christian Missionary Society).

Vedder, Henry C. *A Short History of Baptist Missions*. Philadelphia: The Judson Press, 1927.

Verbeck, G.F. "History of Protestant Missions in Japan," *Proceedings of the General Conference of the Protestant Missionaries of Japan, Osaka, April, 1883*. Yokohama: R. Meiklejohn and Co., 1883.

Wach, Joachim. *Sociology of Religion*. Chicago: The University of Chicago Press, 1944.

Watanabe, Zenta. *Kaishin To Sono Zengo* (The Before and After of Conversion). Tokyo: The Publication Department of the United Church of Christ in Japan, 1957.

Wynd, William. *Seventy Years in Japan: A Saga of Northern Baptists*. New York: The American Baptist Foreign Mission Society, c. 1943.

Yoneda, Isamu. *Nakada Jyuji Den* (Biography of Jyuji Nakada). Tokyo: Nakada Jyuji Den Kanko Kai, 1959.

Young, T.A. "Japan," W.R. Warren (ed.), *Survey of Service, Disciples of Christ*. St. Louis: Christian Board of Publication, 1928.

Zenkoku Kyodo Dendo Iin. (ed.). *Sannen Keizoku Zenkoku Kyodo Dendo* (The Three-Year National Evangelistic Campaign). Tokyo: Fukuin Insatsu Co., Ltd., 1918.

Articles

Brown, Delmer. "Speaking to the New Era: Christians Examine the Future (Christianity and Nationalism)," *The Japan Christian Year Book*, 1968.

Erickson, S.M. "The Problem of Rural Evangelization," *The Chrstian Movement in Japan and Formosa*, 1927.

Fisher, Galen M. "The Missionary Significance of the Last Ten Years: A Survey," *The International Review of Missions*. Vol. 11. April, 1922.

Furuya, Yasuo. "A Review of the Role of Christianity in Japanese Thought," *The Japan Christian Year Book*, 1968.

Iglehart, Charles W. "The Churches in 1931," *The Japan Christian Year Book*, 1932.

International Review of Missions, The. "The Missionary Significance of the Last Ten Years: A Survey." Vol. 21 (1932).

Jaeckel, Theodore. "Japan's Spiritual Situation," *The Japan Christian Quarterly*. Vol. XXI. No. 3. July, 1955.

Kudo, Eiichi. "Shodai Nihon Protesutanto no Shakaiso" (Social Class of Early Protestants in Japan). *The Meiji-Gakuin Ronso*. No. 30. October, 1953.

McKenzie, D.R. "National Evangelistic Campaign," *The Christian Movement in Japan*, 1917.

Masuoka, Jitsuichi. "Urbanization and the Family in Japan," *Sociology and Social Research*. Vol. 32. 1947-48.

Nida, Eugene A. "Culture and Church Growth," *Practical Anthropology*. Vol. 12. No. 1. January-February, 1965.

Passin, Herbert. "The Sources of Protest in Japan," *American Political Science Review*. Vol. 56. June, 1962.

Smith, R.J. "The Japanese Rural Community: Norms, Sanctions, and Ostracism," *American Anthropologist*. 63. ii. Pt. 1. 1961.

Warren, C.M. "The Unreached in the Country and the Gospel Message," *Japan Evangelist*. XXIX. September, 1922.

Unpublished Material

Chee, Changboh. "Development of Sociology in Japan: the Japanese Social Structure." Unpublished Ph.D. dissertation, Duke University, 1959.

Cogswell, James A. "A History of the Work of the Japan Mission of the Presbyterian Church in the United States, 1885-1960." Unpublished Th.D. dissertation, Union Theological Seminary, Richmond, Va., 1961.

Copeland, Edwin Luther. "The Crisis of Protestant Missions to Japan, 1889-1900." Unpublished Ph.D. dissertation, Yale University, 1949.

Floyd, Arva Colbert. "The Founding of the Japan Methodist Church." Unpublished Ph.D. dissertation, Yale University, 1939.

Ikado, Fujio. "The Middle Class and Japanese Protestantism: A Socio-Historical Study of Mission Problems, Especially in Relation to Mission Schools." Unpublished B.D. thesis, The University of Chicago, 1958.

McGovern, James R. "American Christian Missions to Japan, 1918-1941." Unpublished Ph.D. dissertation, University of Pennsylvania, 1957.

Mutch, Robert Bruce. "Channing Moore Williams; First Anglican Bishop of Yedo." Unpublished M.A. thesis, Columbia University, 1966.

Sugii, Mutsuro. "Meiji Oyobi Taisho Zenhanki Nihon Protesutantism No Ichi Kosatsu" (A Study of Japanese Protestantism in the Meiji and the First Half of Taisho Periods). Unpublished manuscript.

Takenaka, Masao. "Relation of Protestantism to Social Problems in Japan, 1900-1941." Unpublished Ph.D. dissertation, Yale University, 1954.

Thomas, Winburn T. "A History of Protestant Christianity in Japan." Unpublished Ph.D. dissertation, Yale University, 1942.

Wright, Morris J. "Survey and Growth Evaluation of the Japan Baptist Convention, 1950-1960." Unpublished D.R.E. dissertation, Southwestern Baptist Theological Seminary, 1961.

Other Sources

Cogswell, James A. Letter to the writer (February 9, 1962).

Matsudaira, Itaro. Letter to the writer (March 6, 1962).

Millard, F.R. Letter to the writer (March 5, 1962).

Thomas, Winburn T. Letter to Donald McGavran (March 19, 1962).

Woodruff, M. Dorothy. Letter to the writer (March 20, 1962).

Yamamori, Tetsunao. An interview with the Holiness leaders conducted in the home of Rev. Tosaji Obara in Tokyo on February 14, 1969. Persons interviewed were Rev. Akiji Kurumada, Rev. Yutaka Yoneda, and Rev. Tosaji Obara.

275.2
Y19
c.2

87534

LINCOLN CHRISTIAN COLLEGE AND SEMINARY

275.2 Y19   c.2
Yamamori, Tetsunao, 1937-
Church growth in Japan

DEMCO

3 4711 00169 6303